THE FIFTH REVOLUTION
A New Agenda for America

Six simple steps toward making America what the

Founding Fathers' intended!

By Richard C Roose

author@thefifthrevolution.org

http://thefifthrevolution.org/forum

Edited by Lynne Vigue

Dedication

This book is dedicated to my children Richard, Gary, Gail, Jerry and Omar; and to their beautiful mothers, Grace, Barbara and Olivia. They paid the highest price for whatever little wisdom I have acquired in my lifetime.

Acknowledgements

I would like to express my appreciation and enduring affection for Lynne Vigue for her skillful editing of the manuscript. I would also like to thank Carol Perkins, Bud Fisher and Denis Basak for proofreading the manuscript and for all of their inputs and conversations during the writing of the manuscript. Without the help of these four people, this book would not have been published.

Disclaimer

This book contains only my opinions; and what I perceive to be the justifications for them. In this book, I propose a New Agenda for Americans and a Purpose of Life for all Humanity; a purpose that will complement the Purpose stated in the Declaration of Independence. I hope this little book will be taken as one side of a conversation; a conversation which you can join by sending an e-mailing to the author (author@thefifthrevolution.org) or by joining The Fifth Revolution at (http:// thefifthrevolution.org/forum/).

Table of Contents

The Fifth Great Earth Revolution - Wisdom

The operating definition of wisdom is as follows: (copied from http://en.wikipedia.org/wiki/Wisdom)

"Wisdom is a deep understanding and realizing of people, things, events or situations, resulting in the ability to choose or act to consistently [to] produce the optimum results with a minimum of time and energy. It is the ability to optimally (effectively and efficiently) apply perceptions and knowledge and so produce the desired results. Wisdom is also the comprehension of what is true or right coupled with optimum judgment as to action. Synonyms include sagacity, discernment, or insight. *Wisdom often requires control of one's emotional reactions (the "passions") so that one's principles, reason and knowledge prevail to determine one's actions.*"

I consider the italicized sentence to express the most crucial aspect of the application of "wisdom." Control of emotion in arriving at judgments is perhaps the element most indicative of a wise person. When I say "control," I do not mean, "suppress" because the emotions are a great part of the intellect. Emotions tell us what we like and what we think is good or bad. Usually following the emotion is a wise course.

The Fifth Revolution will be the last Great Revolution on Earth because all of the Great Revolutions succeeding the Fifth will be extraterrestrial events that will take place on other planets orbiting other suns.

The Fifth Revolution will be characterized by worldwide abandonment of petty and divisive conflict, religious fanaticism, racial hatred, and pursuit of self-interest to the detriment of others. Humankind will exchange these divisive habits for more enlightened (i.e. More "wise") pursuits.

Future historians will characterize the period following the Fifth Revolution as the "Age of Wisdom." As the Fifth Revolution unfolds, more and more human beings will acquire the necessary wisdom for understanding that maximizing individual self-interest can best be accomplished by maximizing the best interests of society. War will be regarded as morally abhorrent-- never justifiable. The manufacture of war materials will cease and the turning of swords into ploughshares will become a worldwide phenomenon. Widespread hunger and disease will be relics of history. Crime and political corruption for monetary profit will cease, and crimes of passion will become rare exceptions to the rule of peaceful coexistence. All humans, regardless of their place of birth or the color of their skin, will be regarded with the dignity that is their birthright. All children will be born into a world that loves and cherishes them as humanity's most precious resource.

Child abuse, a primary cause of human suffering, will no longer be tolerated nor practiced by human beings. As a result, virtually no child anywhere will ever suffer its devastating consequences. Global warming and the destruction of the Earth's environment will cease and its effects will be reversed: Our planet will return to the natural paradise it once was. With the coming of the Fifth Revolution, Earth and all of the efforts and aspirations of its human inhabitants will be guided by wisdom rather than by ignorance and destructive passion, both of which have been all too common throughout human history.

I am not suggesting a utopian fantasy, but rather goals that can be realized, providing all humans accept them as their own. Lest you consider this impossible, I will elucidate five events which have occurred in the last fifty years or so, events which seemed impossible dreams during most of human history. I believe these events foreshadow the coming Revolution.

1. The emancipation of women and growing racial tolerance. For most of human history, a most valuable source of human intelligence and wisdom has been devalued or ignored. Historically, women have been excluded from the halls of political and financial power. Since the founding of our nation, racial bigotry has characterized American society. One need only consider the most recent presidential election of 2008 to realize that much progress has already been made in eliminating these social injustices. In 2008, for the first time in our nation's history, both a woman and a black man were serious candidates for the highest, most powerful political office in the world...and the African-American man was elected! Had any American in 1950 predicted the possibility of such a political eventuality a little over a half century into the future, they would have been disregarded as utopian dreamers.

2. The rise of democracy. In 1944, only 67 years ago, the vast majority of humans on this Earth were subject to a dictatorial or colonial ruler. All of Western Europe was controlled by Nazi fascism. Part of Europe and the northern part of Asia (including parts of China) were ruled by communist dictatorships. The remainder of China was controlled by a military dictatorship and was ruled by warlords. Most of the Pacific region, Indochina and a large part of China were subject to Japanese dictatorship. Almost all of Africa was subject to colonial rule while almost all of South and Latin America were subject to military or colonial rule. Today, totalitarian rule exists in only a handful of nations on Earth; a large portion of the world's population participates in some form of democracy.

3. The rise in human longevity. In 1900, the average human life span in an industrialized nation was less than 45 years. In non-industrialized nations life expectancy was less than 35 years. Today the average human life span is over 72 years. By the end of this century, life expectancy could surpass 100 years. Although the young are sometimes oblivious to the fact, one of the benefits of increasing age is increasing wisdom (even if many seniors often don't act accordingly!) As we age, we tend to discard the passions of youth for a more rational and realistic perspective. It is perhaps because industrialized societies fail to recognize the valuable resource of experientially acquired wisdom that the voices of seniors are so seldom sought or heard. Often, the wisdom possessed by the elderly can be traced to lessons learned in youth, and perhaps many elderly are understandably reluctant to discuss their youthful mistakes.

4. The computer. The computer is such a revolutionary innovation that it has been suggested that we are experiencing a computer revolution of a magnitude comparable to the Industrial Revolution. I disagree. In my opinion, the computer is simply an extension of the printing press. This is not to devalue the computer, for with its added capabilities beyond those of the printing press, the computer is indeed a revolutionary tool. The truly innovative aspect of the computer lies in the fact that it enhances the power of our minds, just as mechanical and electrical tools enhance our muscular power.

While our other tools amplify the power of our muscles as much as a million-fold, allowing us to lift enormously heavy objects, the computer amplifies the power of our minds many million-fold, allowing us to acquire knowledge and accomplish mental tasks with unprecedented accuracy and speed.

5. The explosion of knowledge. It has been estimated by those cognizant of such things that human knowledge doubles every 5 years. Human knowledge implies an understanding of human nature and the workings of the universe. Since understanding the mechanisms of nature implies the capability to intervene for our own purposes, enhanced knowledge implies greater control of our destiny. Assuming that our knowledge has doubled every 5 years for the past 100 years, we now know 1,000,000 times more about our universe than we did 100 years ago! We now know much, much more than our grandparents knew, which provides us with many enhanced powers to control our futures as compared to our parents' parents. If this continues, our grandchildren will know 1,000,000 times more than we do, and will be that much more capable of controlling their futures.

I believe the human race already possesses the knowledge and capability for bringing us much closer to the utopian like paradise I described previously. I believe this because, contained within the knowledge humanity has acquired over the past few hundred years lays a single nugget of truth, a solitary reality so revolutionary, so powerful and yet so fundamental that once realized and fully appreciated, will alter the course of human history towards a more wise, more just, and more progressive destiny. This single fact answers mankind's most meaningful question; an answer that has been sought continuously since the dawn of human cognition. It is an answer humans have sought in vain, an answer that remained elusive for more than 2 million years. Although most people have long believed that the answer to this question was revealed to them, this revealed answer has sometimes proven detrimental to the well-being of human societies. Nevertheless, humankind has based every civilization that has ever existed since the beginning of recorded history on this unsatisfactory answer. Insofar as human civilizations have failed...and they have failed greatly...we can blame these failures on one simple fact: In the absence of knowledge that exists today, past civilizations have been based on the wrong answer to mankind's most important question.

The question mankind has been pondering, the answer to which he has been seeking since the dawn of humanity is "Why am I here?" (i.e. What is the Purpose of My Life?) Humanity finally has enough knowledge to answer the questions!

Introduction

I begin this book by summarizing my entire hypotheses in a few paragraphs. I have entitled my theories "The Fifth Revolution," which will follow the first four revolutions of "Life", "Intelligence", "Agriculture", and "Industry". I believe that The Fifth Revolution will consist of the acquisition of "Wisdom" by the vast majority of the earth's human population. Thus, "Wisdom" represents the next step in the evolution of life on planet Earth.

The founding fathers very clearly stated the National purpose of the United States of America in the second and last sentences of the Declaration of Independence…

> Second sentence
>
> "We hold these truths to be self-evident, that all men are created equal, that they are endowed by their Creator with certain unalienable Rights, that among these are Life, Liberty and the pursuit of Happiness."
>
> Last sentence
>
> "And for the support of this Declaration, with a firm reliance on the protection of the Divine Providence, we mutually pledge to each other our Lives, our Fortunes, and our sacred Honor."

This stated purpose has served America well throughout the eras of the Revolutionary War, the Civil War and two great World Wars. Accomplishment of any goal presupposes a purpose or reason for doing so. Accordingly, a common purpose is necessary for the leadership and citizens of any nation to fulfill their nation's promise. As history has demonstrated when our citizens unite in a common cause, our potential for accomplishing whatever we desire is virtually unlimited.

My main premise and my motivations for advancing that premise are...

I believe that everyone has multiple purposes and multiple instincts which drive these purposes. No one acts without purpose, whether that purpose is stated, implied or subconscious. For example, the purpose of work is to provide food and shelter for oneself and one's family. The purpose of watching a football game is enjoyment. The purpose of sex is two-fold: enjoyment of the act and procreation. Often, the latter is an undesired result of the first!

My basic hypotheses are...

> 1. Within the foreseeable future, humanity will be forced to address some very vital problems...problems which, if not adequately solved, could result in the extinction of all humanity. I believe the proper solution to these most vital issues necessarily entails radical changes in the conduct of American affairs.

> 2. I see no evidence for hope that the necessary radical changes are being contemplated or implemented anywhere on our planet. The fact is that the overwhelming problems facing America today cannot and will not be solved until they are attacked on a common front by all Americans working within a common agenda.

> 3. From my research and observation of the reality of the human condition (including any and all issues which impact human existence), I

have concluded that there are only six aspects of American affairs which require radical change. I will discuss these crucial issues in succeeding chapters.

4. My long years of research and observation have also convinced me that the most difficult problem facing the human race is the abuse and improper rearing of children by their parents, who are often well-meaning but who lack a proper understanding of the solution to mankind's most urgent question. I believe that child abuse, both physical and psychical, is responsible for most of the injustice and immorality that regretfully exists in our modern world.

5. Child abuse because of parental ignorance is one aspect of the human condition that can be radically altered: We need only recognize the crucial need for educating our children with respect to wise parenting and the art of wisdom long before they reach reproductive age.

6. Effecting this radical change to the educational system (in conjunction with the other 5 necessary changes) will be impossible unless there is an explicit "national agenda" in that regard. This would require that a majority of all American citizens agree with the wisdom of such changes, since nationwide consensus cannot be achieved without acknowledgement of a common national agenda.

7. I believe that most Americans already accept (whether consciously or subconsciously) that the primary purpose and responsibility of humanity is the unconditional love, care,

nourishment and education of their children. Thus, a declaration of this as our national purpose and perhaps even the law of the land would raise consciousness as to its vital importance for our future prosperity,

In order to establish these seven areas of change, which I believe are vital to the survival of humanity beyond the next 200 years, I propose the following:

1. A Nation wide, majority acknowledgement and agreement as to the "New National Agenda of America." (i.e. the unconditional love, care, nourishment and education of American children.) This will be an agenda that complements the stated National purpose as defined by the founding fathers in the Declaration of Independence some 235 years ago.

2. Establishment within our public education system of curricula requiring the teaching of the art of wise parenting and the teaching of the art of wisdom. So that our children may understand from an early age that parenting is the most important and difficult task they will undertake in adulthood; thereby conveying to them that wise parenting and wisdom are crucial to societal health and prosperity of America.

3. Abandonment of the counter productive notion that the purpose of government is to "rule". In reality, governments should exist to facilitate a public forum for the safe, just, moral and efficient conduct of social interaction.

4. Minimizing crime by eliminating the exchange of currency. Since most Americans living today have largely abandoned the practice

of conducting business through cash exchange in favor of the electronic transfer of funds, this is certainly not an unrealistic proposal.

5. Prison reform aimed at reinforcing the primary role of corrective facilities as institutions for rehabilitation, rather than as breeding grounds for further criminal behavior upon release of the criminal

6. Elimination of the National "debt."

7. A more just distribution of wealth in United States and, eventually, throughout the world.

Human Education

Perhaps the most insidious consequence of bad parenting is that mistakes made in the raising of one generation are passed onto succeeding generations. Parents may have the best of intentions, but never having been educated in the art of good parenting, their efforts prove inadequate. Most parents acquire the bulk of their parenting skills via observation and experience with their own parents. Largely, the art of raising children is acquired through "on the job training" (i.e. OJT). As a result, many parents abuse their children in ways they do not intend. This unintentional abuse is the leading cause of the injustice, immorality and unhappiness that exists in human society. We can halt the propagation of abuse from generation to generation by simply educating public school children in the wisdom of parenting and the proper art of raising their future offspring.

The most crucial aspect of fulfilling the Purpose of Life lies in educating children with regard to proper parenting. Through education, we provide our children with the knowledge, the beliefs, and the tools required for shaping the next generation, as well as all future generations for centuries to come.

I cannot conceive of a nobler, more important, or more enduring application of our knowledge, our wealth, and our resources than the proper education of children in the art of nurturing.

Most failures of past civilizations have their roots in the improper education of children. Children have been inadequately educated in human knowledge, yet strongly encouraged to embrace faith based on ancient myths and fables rather than on scientifically verifiable reality. The primary objective of education has been to mold children so that they will conform to local cultural beliefs and practices. Of course, many of the past deficits in early education were due to simple lack of knowledge about the workings of the universe. Another and perhaps more important reason is that faith in the prevailing religion was one mechanism whereby the ruling class controlled society and propagated itself.

Vestiges of improper education from past civilizations still exist in the prevalence and popularity of fairy tales in children's literature. Fairy tales wrongly convey to children that magic is a component of the workings of the universe. Magical possibilities continue to be accepted into adulthood, as these are necessary components for religious belief. If children are given the impression at a very early age that magic is real, religious beliefs will seem plausible to them as adults. In reality, fantasy and magic are forbidden by the Laws of Nature, as we currently understand them.

If we are to educate our children properly, it is absolutely vital that we educate them in the Truth, the whole Truth and nothing but the Truth, as best we humans can possibly know that Truth. If we convey falsehoods to our children, whether intentionally or as a result of ignorance, we may preclude them from ever realizing the truth, as it will be obscured in falsehood. In conveying falsehoods to our children, we empower them to perpetrate the same mistruths, in direct contradiction to the morality we are trying to convey to them at the same time. When we convey falsehoods to our children, we are preventing them from ever reaching their full potential as human beings. When we convey falsehoods to our children, we are creating flaws in the fabric of the next generation of society, flaws that may be perpetuated for many generations.

The worst possible strategy for raising children is the "do as I say, not as I do" approach. Children have a very powerful and instinctual "BS" detector. They disdain any form of hypocrisy. This is, perhaps, an important reason why children often disobey their parents: they do not trust their parents because they believe their parents have lied to them!

The best possible way to educate children is by example. It is an important component of the inborn instinct of children to imitate their parents. This means that parents must live the manner they want their children to live. If a child's total experience can be defined by unconditional love, honesty, honor, purpose, persistence, diligence, dedication, self-sufficiency, self-confidence and self-control, that child will most likely grow into an adult who exhibits those same character strengths.

Moreover, a person whose character is so described is almost by definition a happy person, no matter his or her circumstances in life!

Wouldn't it be wonderful if every human child could grow into such an adult? Who would not want this for their own children?

Because children learn 90% of everything they will ever learn by the age of five, the first five years of education are the most important (i.e. Critical) years of the child's education. We know this is so because the human child's brain grows to 90% of its adult size by age five or six. The growth of the brain is due to the addition and interconnections of neurons that form as the child learns. This critical period for the creation of neurons and their interconnections accounts for the crucial importance of the early years of any child's life.

The two persons most often responsible for the first crucial years of a child's education are, of course, the mother and father of the child. Nevertheless, most parents are completely unaware of the mechanisms whereby infants learn. Most new parents are not cognizant of the most important information the infant will learn, whether purposely taught or not, nor of the primary manner in which infants learn their most important lessons. This is a most significant educational deficit: People must learn how to be good parents before they become parents.

Teaching children how to be good parents should and *must* be the primary objective of all education. This education should commence during the critical first five years of a child's life and is best conveyed by the example of good parenting. The training of children after the first five years must continue with the primary objective of teaching children the techniques of successful parenting, as this is the best strategy for insuring success in the pursuit of the National Agenda. Unless children mature into adults with the knowledge, ability, capability, and sincere desire to become ideal parents to their children, they are doomed to failure. No human can successfully practice that of which he is not fully cognizant.

Since perfection is not humanly possible, it is most important that human education after the first five years include reversing errors made by parents during the first five years of each child's life. Such education might offend many parents who were misled to believe by their own parents, that their personal methods of childrearing were ideal. Many people believe that children turn out to be good or bad adults simply because it is in the child's nature to be good or bad. This fallacy has taken root in human societies and has been perpetuated by misguided and misinformed education! In reality, the nature/nurture dichotomy is a myth: nature and nurture interact in the development of any child. Without nature, no child could exist. Without nurture, no child could develop and learn.

If we are to establish the most ideal educational system possible, we must *correct the misconception* that parents can do little to influence the adults their children will become. In order to overcome this obstacle, two facts must be realized as absolute.

1. Human children are born with primitive reflexes for survival. Newborns possess absolutely no knowledge or inclination beyond this instinctual urge. Newborns are aware of only two sensations, comfort and discomfort. These two perceptions, interacting with their inborn nature and their life experiences, develop naturally into the full range of emotions the individual will experience throughout life. Everything any human can or will ever be, everything any human can or will do is shaped and altered by experiences and the emotions that develop because of those experiences. They will strive for and be attracted to those experiences that provide comfort; they will avoid and be repelled by experiences that give them discomfort. Every individual human quickly learns the kinds of experiences that bring comfort and the kinds of experience that bring discomfort. Parents must strive to give their children only the kinds of experiences that bring them comfort.

2. The worst possible mistruth we can convey to our children is that we, the parent, know with absolute certainty anything at all beyond the Laws of Nature. We must not mislead children into believing that our or our parents, methods of childrearing are the ideal strategies, for in so doing we are discouraging them from seeking better methodologies. In fact, it is simply impossible for us to know with certainty anything

beyond our logical and scientific understanding of the Laws of Nature. All beliefs beyond this consist of conjectures and imaginings that differ from culture to culture. The only concrete and absolute Truth that exists in the Universe are the Laws of Nature. It is most important that we educate our children in the Laws of Nature as they are currently understood, including (and perhaps most importantly) the fact that our knowledge of these Laws is incomplete. We must teach our children that it is their responsibility to endeavor to enhance our knowledge of the Laws of Nature, as well as to seek new and improved methods for accomplishing life goals. We should not desire, as has been the wish of all human societies in the past, that our children inherit our own limitations. On the contrary, we should hope that they would surpass us in every meaningful aspect, providing them with an enhanced ability to address their own problems and the problems of society in general.

The fundamental objective of human education must be to provide children with the knowledge and means to accomplish the National Agenda, (i. e., the proper raising and education of their children.) We can best accomplish this goal by instilling in children the capability for giving and receiving unconditional love, by encouraging the characteristics of honesty, honor, purpose, persistence, diligence, dedication, self-sufficiency, self-confidence and self-control, and by providing our children with a sound appreciation for and understanding of the Laws of Nature. In other words, we must teach children how to be just, moral, happy, successful and productive citizens of society. Furthermore, we must train children to avoid repeating the mistakes of previous generations.

Parenting in America

The most important truth any parent should know is that the need for unconditional love is a powerful and primary human instinct. Unconditional love is both a compelling emotion and a powerful motivator. It is vital to the growth and development of children, while parental withholding of unconditional love can have devastating consequences on their children. See (http://umaine.edu/publications/4356e/)

Unconditional love can trump even the survival instinct. We know this is so because parents will deliberately risk their own lives in order to protect the children they love unconditionally.

(For a more in-depth reading of human instincts and emotions see "Maslow's hierarchy of needs" (http://en.wikipedia.org/wiki/Maslow's_hierarchy_of_n eeds).

Unconditional love is, as the phrase implies, love without conditions. Parents who love unconditionally place no conditions, qualifications, or requirements on their love. Their children are loved by virtue of their very existence. Unconditional love does not waver. Unconditional love remains steadfast even under the most trying of circumstances, and especially during adolescence, when children often express contempt for the parents who stand in the way of their independence.

Parents must love unconditionally, because raising children is a serious responsibility, and even the most obedient and agreeable children will occasionally try the patience of the most devoted parent! Moreover, love is required from the instant a child is born, and often begins well before birth. As many mothers will attest, unconditional, life-altering love can be felt the moment the pregnancy is confirmed! It would hardly be conducive to human survival if parental love had to develop and grow as the parents became acquainted with their offspring.

Unconditional love may be tenacious and self-sacrificing, but not all forms of tenacious and self-sacrificing love are unconditional. Certainly, the all-consuming emotion that characterizes romantic lovers can be so powerful that a lover would be willing to sacrifice his or her own life for the sake of their beloved. Soldiers in battle often risk their lives in order to save their buddies. However, neither forms of love are truly unconditional, since they do not arise instantaneously once the existence of the beloved becomes known to the lover.

Most non-parental loving relationships require a "getting acquainted" period during which personal qualities and characteristics of the future friends or lovers become apparent. It may be true that in rare circumstances, love that begins as conditional becomes unconditional, meaning that there are no circumstances under which it would be withdrawn. There are many stories of doomed love, in which one of the partners falls out of love, while the other simply cannot stop loving the object of his affection no matter how cruelly he is treated, or how firmly his love is rejected.

However, divorce rates and the frequent estrangement of former friends are testimony to the fact that such forms of love only rarely become unconditional.

On the other hand, the relative rarity of cases in which children are disowned by their own parents demonstrates that parental love is more likely to be unconditional than other, less enduring of love. The difficulties that often arise between step parents and their step children is further evidence that the bonds of unconditional love are more easily forged very early in the life of the child.

How does unconditional love develop in infants? We know that newborns have no awareness of their own existence, their emotions, or their motivations. Human beings are born in a psychically primitive state, requiring interaction with the world in order for their consciousness to fully develop. Thus, newborns are not aware of loving or being loved. We cannot, of course, know exactly what a newborn "feels" since they cannot communicate with us and accurate memories of that stage of life do not persist until humans are capable of communication. In other words, we cannot know if newborns experience a primitive form of love, but can be fairly confident that, if so, they aren't aware of having that experience.

Human infants are born with powerful instincts for survival in place. The infant crying reflex ensures that mothers are aware when babies are hungry or experiencing discomfort. The rooting and swallowing reflexes allow human infants to nurse, thereby obtaining vital nutrition for growth.

It is only later, as infants experience parental affection and nurturing, that conscious emotions develop. The parental bond develops as parents unconditionally love their babies, and the object of their affection returns that love with steadfast devotion. The love of small children for their parents is as unconditional as love can be; even children who have been severely abused by their parents will strongly resist being separated from those abusive parents.

It is often stated that infants perceive themselves as the center of the universe. Since the unconditional love of their parents represents confirmation of this misconception, young children constantly seek parental attention and parental approval. Small children readily sense parental moods, and thus are happiest when they sense happiness in their parents. On the other hand, they can also be greatly unsettled by parental disapproval or unhappiness.

Through the experience of unconditional love, and to the extent it is truly unconditional, the child learns to accept and to receive this love, and matures into adulthood with both capacities. Parents whose interactions with their own parents were characterized by unconditional love will, in turn, forge these bonds with their own children. Similarly, children who have been denied unconditional love in their formative years will be handicapped with respect to their relationships, including and most importantly, their relationships with their own children. *Parents who withhold unconditional love deny their children the necessary foundation for a healthy and happy emotional life in adulthood.*

Thus, it is of vital importance to the future of our descendants, our country, and our species that parents learn how to give and receive this most powerful, most noble, and most crucial of all emotions.

The best method for learning good parenting is by following the example of one's own parents. Imitating their mother is the primary way girls learn to be mothers and imitating their father is the primary way boys learn to be fathers.

The best possible way to educate children is by example. It is part of the inborn instinct of children to imitate their parents. Thus, parents must live the way they would like their children to live. If parents demonstrate only *unconditional love, honesty, honor, purpose, persistence, diligence, dedication, self-*

sufficiency, self-confidence and *self-control*, their children will become adults capable of giving unconditional love, and they will most likely manifest the characteristics of honesty, honor, purpose, persistence, diligence, dedication, self-sufficiency, self-confidence and self-control. Additionally, such a person is almost by definition a happy person, regardless of their circumstances in life.

Are these characteristics not viewed as virtuous by all human societies?

Many, upon reading this formula for good parenting, will question the plausibility of such a seemingly idealistic scenario. Actually, it is not a hopeless fantasy that children can learn perfect parenting. While it is true that humans are limited by imperfect knowledge, it is also true that humans can acquire the necessary knowledge to become better parents. Unless we understand and embody the characteristics necessary in order to become a "Good Parent," our children will be incapable of learning those characteristics by our example. Thus, this chapter is devoted to methods for conveying strategies for good parenting to our children. After all, conveying methods for good parenting to succeeding generations is the purpose of this book, this life, and this universe!

What I am suggesting is instructing our public school students, from kindergarten to graduation, in the same characteristics that U.S Marine enlistees (largely unruly teenagers from poor families) are expected to learn in merely 13 weeks of boot camp training. We have 13 years to accomplish the same task. Surely, persons who have devoted their lives to the proper education of children can devise primary and secondary curricula that will prove even more effective than the U.S. Marines' tactics for instilling the personal characteristics required for excellence in parenting: honesty, honor, purpose, persistence, diligence, dedication, self-sufficiency, self-confidence and self control.

In addition to these personal character traits, there are other requirements for good parenting:

1. Applying and exhibiting wisdom in every significant decision we make!

2. Achieving financial stability and providing sufficient income, capital, and insurance to care for one's family. Employment for at least one parent is thus a requirement in virtually all families.

3. Acquiring sufficient education to understand and take advantage of new technical developments, to analyze reports of local, national and international events, and to understand history as it relates to current events. Educated parents are, of course, better prepared to provide proper answers to their children's endless "why" questions. Educating oneself in both knowledge and the most efficient means to acquire it are prerequisites for raising well informed children.

4. Awareness of the danger of transmitting harmful genetic diseases to future generations. If couples who jointly show a high probability of producing children with debilitating or lethal genetic diseases refrained from bearing children, or sought alternative methods for parenting (i.e. Adoption, artificial insemination, in vitro fertilization or surrogate parenting), they could eliminate their chances of bearing severely impaired offspring.

Any individual who possesses the above qualifications, who can provide unconditional love, and who manifests the characteristics of honesty, honor, purpose, persistence, diligence, dedication, self-sufficiency, self-confidence and self-control, is properly qualified to become a good parent. Without these qualifications and characteristics, the best one can expect is poor or inadequate parenting. It is a fact that most mothers and fathers became parents without having been educated in the art of good parenting. In all too many cases, parents damage their children's self-image well into adulthood. Such children may be so impaired that they are hampered to varying degrees in their later social interactions. No doubt, there are many adults who have been victims of improper parenting in society today, and these dysfunctional adults are responsible for many of our social ills, including the great disparity between human social classes. In general, the most dysfunctional occupy the lower levels of our social strata. All too often, those on the lower rungs of the social ladder are incapable of escaping their lot.

If we recognize that most humans are deficient to some degree in parenting skills and that parenting is the most crucial occupation that any human will undertake, it becomes obvious that we must transform the curricula of our schools in order to correct any inadequacies in their students' pre-school experiences with respect to parenting.

Of course, the most serious impediment to this plan lies in the fact that very few parents wish to face their own inadequacies. Moreover, parents would almost certainly be reluctant to allow the public school system to suggest to their children that they have been the victims of improper or inadequate pre-school parenting! I realize that this revolution cannot take place in one generation, and that no one can change the world in a single lifetime. Yet, even the longest journeys must begin with a single step.

I sincerely hope that the living generations of humanity include an adequate proportion of persons with sufficient wisdom to establish at least a few pilot schools based on the principles suggested in this book.

I hope that, because of the success these schools will enjoy, others will take note and seek the same for their own children. No doubt, this educational revolution will proceed slowly at the beginning, and will gain momentum until the success rate of the system's graduates is so significant that those not employing the new system will be relatively disadvantaged. I hope that, eventually, the entire world will adopt the system I have outlined in this book. Then within one generation of its having been achieved, it will receive worldwide recognition.

The Teaching Computer

Second only to the "printing press," the "computer" is the greatest invention in human history. In fact, the computer's impact on human progress may actually surpass that of the printing press. Much like all tools, the computer "amplifies" human capabilities, allowing its users to accomplish far more tasks with much, much greater speed than would be possible without it. Eyeglasses, magnifying glasses, microscopes and telescopes amplify our visual perception by orders of magnitude greater than would be possible without them. Hearing aids literally amplify sound for the hearing impaired. Other machines enable the lifting and moving of objects much larger and heavier than would otherwise be humanly possible, even for a large group of humans working together. At best, even a very powerful human can throw a stone only a few hundred feet into the air, while our rocket launchers can heave battleships into orbit around the Earth, and dispatch robot probes to other planets in the solar system.

The computer is an instrument that amplifies the most powerful and important capability humanity possesses: human brainpower. This tool of the human mind will continue to improve, enhancing human mental capacities even further. Thus, the computer will facilitate improvement in the human condition to a degree that cannot be imagined by even the most futuristic minds of today, and it will be an indispensable tool for human advancement until the end of human existence. The vital significance of the computer to human societal progress cannot be overstated.

The Teaching Computer (TC) will represent one of the most important information technological developments in the 21st century, if not the most important. The TC is already in the early developmental stages, and most of the technologies necessary for its implementation already exist. Teaching computers will appear similar to the laptop computers already familiar to us, but they will have far greater capabilities, particularly with respect to power, speed, memory capacity, graphics, human interface and security. Actually, the TC's hardware will be nothing more than a very powerful general-purpose computer applicable to almost any computer task. What will distinguish the TC from other general-purpose computers is the software that will be installed and implemented on it.

The software for the TC will be developed specifically to enable its use as the most perfect "teaching tutor" conceivable by human imagination. This will allow the TC to tutor its student users on any subject within human knowledge or imagination in a format that is most conducive to presenting each subject. Moreover, the lessons will be implemented in a manner that is perfectly compatible with the previous education and skill levels of the student: The TC will automatically adjust its lessons to the aptitude and attitude of its student users, tailoring each individualized lesson to the student's current level of achievement, as well as to his particular interests and learning capabilities.

Through the internet, the TC will make available to every child on Earth the totality of all useful human knowledge. Furthermore, the TC will automatically protect impressionable children from negative influences such as pornographic or violence-promoting sites, and other sites which society deems unacceptable for consumption by children. Perhaps a special internet for children can be developed for use with the TC only.

The graphic capability of the TC will allow lessons to be presented as "3D virtual reality," allowing the student to become a virtual and integral part of the lesson. For example, history could be presented from the viewpoint of the major participants in historical events. Abraham Lincoln's virtual self could be employed to personally inform students of his thoughts, emotions, and motivations with respect to the civil war. Participants of great battles who fought and died on both sides could relate their experiences, much as a grandfather might relate to his grandchildren historical events he had personally witnessed. Science education in chemistry or physics could be presented as if the student were an integral part of each experiment, witnessing the movements and changes of a particular molecule in a chemical reaction, or the progress of a falling body as it increases in speed until it reaches orbital velocity. Math could be taught as animated numbers that depict the operations of addition, subtraction, multiplication and division. The possibilities for presenting a variety of different lessons are limited only by human imagination—which is virtually limitless.

The software for the TC will be "open source," much like the Linux operating systems in today's computers. Companies across the world would compete with one another to produce the best and most comprehensive systems for the entire worldwide market. The programming skills required to write TC programs would be widespread talents, allowing millions of the most talented people in the world, including children, to write programs for the TC. The worldwide involvement of the brightest and most talented of the earth's citizens would ensure that the software would always be the latest, best, and most powerful available. Being open source, the software would be inexpensive or perhaps even free for those who could not otherwise afford it.

The TC would allow any child or adult, anywhere on Earth, access to the best education possible. Furthermore, it would allow every student at any level to progress at their own individual pace, and to go virtually anywhere their passionate thirst for knowledge might lead them. The TC would free human teachers from most of the mundane tasks associated with teaching, allowing them to use their social and nurturing skills to encourage each students to progress as far and as fast as possible. No more will the brightest students be held back as the teacher necessarily focuses her attention on the less talented. Teachers would find more time to devote to individual students who require personalized instruction, without risk of boring their more advanced students. Teachers would also have more time for instructing their students in parenting, morality, ethics, personal health, social studies and interpersonal relationships--subjects for which human teachers are better suited than even the most powerful computer ever could be.

Of course, no computer could ever replace a human teacher's empathy, care, and genuine concern for the educational progress and well being of her students. Only a human teacher could detect nuances in her students' thoughts and behavior, nuances that could impact the student's capacity for personal development and/or educational progress. Only a human teacher could provide comfort and solace to a child in emotional distress. Thus, no teacher need ever worry that her job will become obsolete.

The TC will result in a significant reduction in the cost of public education in many ways. Improvements in the teacher to student ratio without increasing expenses and reduction of the hardware that is now required for educating children from kindergarten through high school are but two examples.

A New School System for America

Fifth Revolution, the Age of Wisdom, and the development of a wise human society will be accomplished primarily in the nation's public school systems. This will occur gradually as first private schools and then isolated public school districts develop and adapt curricula for properly educating children in the principals I suggested in the previous chapters.

The most significant difference between these new school curricula and our current courses of study will be in their primary objectives. Instead of the "3R's, (reading, 'riting and 'rithmatic), the new curricula will be characterized by two principle objectives. First will be the education of children in wise parenting; Second will be the correction of errors made by the parents during the pre-school years of their children.

Another important difference between the new schools and the old will be in the operation and staffing of the new schools.

The new school systems will be staffed by more teachers and assistants than is the case in today's schools. The teacher-to-child ratio will approach one adult for each ten students. About one-half of the adult staff will be retired senior citizens and college student volunteers who will function as teacher's aids. Formal class sizes would be limited to ten students, with usually one teacher and one teacher's aid.

The first two years of school would be devoted to teaching children the fundamentals, as is the case today. However, in the new schools there will be with much greater emphasis on computer skills. Each child will have their own personal "Teaching Computer" (TC) as I have described in the previous chapter. Although writing skills and penmanship will be taught as they are today, keyboarding skills will also be included. By the end of its second year, each child will be a fast and skilled typist with a comprehensive understanding of how to use the internet for retrieval of information.

The Teaching Computer will be a very powerful laptop computer, programmed with all courses available at each grade level. The TC will be a marvelous teaching tool with capabilities for presenting each lesson at each child's optimum learning rate. The TC will never tire of searching and finding the most effective methods for presenting different fields of study to the even the most challenged students. Furthermore, the TC will have the capability for detecting and adjusting its lessons according to the individual child's temperament. TC's will be programmed with best and most current teaching methods and skills available. The TC and the Internet will provide every child on Earth with access to the best education humanity can provide, yet it will be affordable to even the poorest child.

After the second year of the new elementary school curriculum, the grade levels will be less distinct than they are currently. The teaching of most subjects will shift from classroom instruction to TC courses. The computer will then serve as an individualized tutor, allowing teachers to concentrate on assisting those students who most require personalized instruction, and on teaching subjects best taught in the traditional manner—subjects such as parenting, morals and interpersonal relationships. Children will be encouraged to proceed through each lesson at their own individualized pace. Children who fall behind will receive sufficient additional instruction to achieve the necessary standards required by the course of study. Gifted and talented children who are capable of learning at an accelerated pace will be encouraged to delve deeper into the subject and to proceed to more advanced topics. Classes will more closely resemble club meetings than traditional methods of instruction. Teachers will lead discussions concerning lessons learned via the TC, and children will be encouraged to ask questions, allowing the teacher to clarify information and to correct misconceptions.

Teacher-student interaction will provide teachers with the means to monitor each student's progress and to provide guidance where it is most needed. It is possible that, in many cases, teacher-student meetings need only occur once or twice a week. Teachers' aids could provide sufficient adult guidance at other times, and the children could tutor each other, much as patients in group therapy help each other. This would not only provide teachers with much more time to tutor the more needy individuals and to communicate with parents; it would also foster a much richer learning environment for the students. Students would be invited to join advanced classes as soon as they achieve the standards required for their particular grade level. Thus, any given class could be composed of members of various ages and grade levels. Talented children who are willing and capable could even complete high school requirements by age 12 or 13 and then proceed to college-level courses.

These new schools will encourage much greater parent participation, and will thus be characterized by greater interaction between teachers and parents. Weekly parent/teacher gatherings will take place, with most parents and teachers attending. At these gatherings, teachers and administrators will present and discuss future school operations, allowing parents to provide feedback on current operations and to suggest new directions. Since, in the beginning, the new schools will be private and/or administered by small public school districts, a significant proportion of parents, facilitating very productive meetings, could attend the gatherings.

Defining a good parent is similar to defining pornography. As a judge once remarked "I don't know what it is, but I know it when I see it."

If we are to teach our children to be good parents, it behooves us to find a proper definition, lest we remain uncertain of how to instruct our children in that most important of all arts.

I define a good parent as...

1. A person who is successful at their chosen profession.

2. A person who is financially stable and capable of providing the necessities of life for their children.

3. A person who is willing and capable of providing unconditional love.

4. A person who displays the habits of honesty, honor, purpose, persistence, diligence, dedication, self-sufficiency, self-confidence and self-control.

5. A person who is able to project these characteristics in every interaction with the child.

How can we convey these ideas to our children? The first component of good parenting is relatively simple. If we provide children with the opportunity for a sound liberal and technical education, they are most likely to become successful in their chosen careers and to achieve the necessary financial stability for supplying their own children's needs. We already know how to do this, as we have been implementing this goal in schools all across the globe for thousands of years. It is in the area of personal character traits that our schools have proven insufficient. How do we discipline and regiment six-year-old children?

We know that most of a child's personality and character are developed during the first six years of the child's life. We also know that if the parent's personality and character include the capability of giving unconditional love and the characteristics of honesty, honor, purpose, persistence, diligence, dedication, self-sufficiency, self confidence and self-control, and if the parent demonstrates those noble character traits in all aspects of their lives, there is a very high probability their children will develop similar character strengths.

Of course, the unpleasant reality is that there are probably none of us who could live up to these standards every day, 24 hours a day. Most of us do not even approach these standards. Why is this the case? It seems most likely that, to the extent that our parents were deficient in the desired personality and character traits, we were hampered in our inability to learn by example from our parents. Acquiring those character traits later in childhood was not an option for most of us, because there were no alternatives to parental instruction and example.

All human beings are born with an incompletely developed central nervous system. If the proper neurons are not triggered to fire and interconnect, and fired with great regularity over the full course of our first five years of life, the missing character traits simply do not become wired into our brains.

Moreover, if negative character traits become established during pre-school development, they supersede and/or weaken connections that would otherwise lead to character strengths. Consider that even the slightest single rejection of an infant by a primary care giver can trigger an interconnection within the brain that could damage that child's self-image to an extent that it might completely override almost all future positive experiences. Any love henceforth heaped upon that child might remain tainted in the infant's perception by that single experience of rejection. Imagine how much more dire the consequences could be if the abuse is constant? Keep in mind that even the slightest rejection of an infant can be rightfully characterized as abuse. The helpless infant most likely develops in a prison of self-loathing, a prison from which he might never escape.

Fortunately, the human brain is a very plastic organ capable of re-wiring itself. Equally fortunate is the fact that severe child abuse is rare in human societies. Thus, it is possible, with proper education and/or medication and therapy, to correct most of the errors parents make during the first five years of their children's lives. Certainly, no parent is perfect, and therefore all parents are guilty of at least some parenting errors.

This is the rationale behind the second objective of the new school system, the reversal of parental mistakes. All teachers in the new school system will be specifically trained to identify and address any problems they observe in their students. All of the children's negative issues will be dealt with according to the severity of the problem. Strategies for dealing with these problems include group therapy, referral to outside resources, and mandatory psychological therapy for both parents and children whenever this is warranted. The idea of our school systems addressing mental health issues may seem abhorrent to some. Bear in mind, however, that initially this curriculum will be implemented in schools and districts in which parents themselves recognize the potential benefits of such an approach for both themselves and their children.

This is why the Teaching Computer will play such an important role in the everyday operation of the new schools. I estimate that teachers in the new schools will spend more than 60% of their time in counselling of and interaction with their students. The TC will allow teachers sufficient free time away from their classrooms for accomplishing these personalized and individualized interactions.

(With over 41 million students, the largest school in the world is the Khan Academy (http://www.khanacademy.org/). This school consist of 2100 videos that cover a broad range of subjects, and eventually will cover almost all possible school subjects. This is the kind of software I foresee for the Teaching Computer. Each lesson is broken down into individual steps so that the student first gets a firm foundation and then goes on in depth into the subject matter. The school is free to anyone who can connect to the Internet. It has been so successful that the Bill Gates Foundation has stepped up to finance the project and Google gave the Khan Academy a $2 million prize for being one of the best ideas to change the world.)

The senior citizen and college student volunteer teachers' aids will also play an important role in the success of the both the school system and its students. These volunteers will be rigorously screened and trained to complement the teachers. So many senior citizens today have much to offer our children, and so many are eager to help. It is truly sad that the wisdom, talents and experiences of our seniors are so readily discounted and devalued in our current youth-oriented culture. I predict that these senior teaching aid positions will be eagerly sought by seniors, and will be so coveted that there will be many more applications than positions available. I also expect that the experience resulting from the college student aid positions will prove so valuable, especially for elementary or secondary education students, that applications for these positions will far exceed available openings as well. In the beginning, the seniors and college students will do much to enlighten the public concerning the successes of the new educational system.

Of course, the inception, growth, and establishment of the new school system will not occur overnight. A few generations of parents who have been educated in parenting in childhood will be required before the full implications of this educational system are realized. Nevertheless, I believe the school system will achieve significant recognition within a relatively short time span, thanks primarily to the obvious success of the system as realized in the successes of its former students. Drug abuse and juvenile delinquency among students in these new schools will be the lowest of any school system in the country, while the overall academic achievement of students from the new schools will be among the highest of all school systems. The crime rate among students of these schools will also be among the lowest in the nation. The system will achieve a high school completion rate in the high 90th percentile, and in some schools or districts will approach 100%. Seventy percent or higher of the new system's graduates will go on to complete college. The personal successes achieved in adulthood by the system's graduates will also be notable, with far fewer failed marriages and much lower rates of health and mental problems. Alcoholism will be rare among graduates, as will be drug abuse and criminal activity.

The cost of this new school system will be relatively inexpensive compared that of our current educational system, especially when one considers the teacher-student ratio. Many of our current educational systems' problems and costs will be eliminated through better management and better control of students. Much of the equipment now regarded as essential for a modern school will be eliminated and replaced by the Teaching Computer and its software. Even classrooms such as chemistry labs will not be necessary for general education students, as students will be able to perform "virtual" experiments on their TCs. As a result, with no risk of dangerous accident, the students will "conduct" more experiments of a more sophisticated nature than students in an actual science laboratory. The smaller class sizes will require less space, and more classrooms will occupy the same physical areas that house a fewer number of classrooms today.

A large component of the new curriculum will be devoted to personal health, including proper nutrition and the avoidance of chemical stimulants. Obesity will be strongly discouraged and the causes of obesity will be thoroughly understood by the students, who will be encouraged to regard the human body as a temple to be revered and never degraded by unhealthy practices. Consequently, the health costs now incurred by both schools and parents will be greatly reduced, as earlier detection of medical problems will result in a healthier student body. Security will also be more easily implemented, thanks to the greater supervision of students allowed by the smaller teacher-to-student ratio. With the extra time afforded by the TC and the additional adult supervision provided by teachers' aids, no area of school grounds will be without adult supervision.

The impressive successes of the new school system will not go unnoticed by the media and thus will be widely reported. For this reason, and for the reasons outlined above, I believe the new school system I am proposing will grow exponentially across the country and will eventually be accepted and perhaps even mandated by federal law. This growth will result from the public's taking notice of the superior education and capabilities of the system's graduates. Widespread adoption of the new system will result in unprecedented economic growth for our country. As the system continues to expand, the high school dropout rate will fall to the lowest in the world, while the percentage of Americans with college and advanced degrees will exceed that of every other nation on Earth by a significant margin. Crime rates, drug abuse, alcoholism and mental health problems will fall to the lowest rate ever experienced by any nation. The overall health of the nation's population will dramatically improve, and health care costs will decrease to the lowest per capital rate of any nation, ever.

Other nations of the world may be inspired to follow our example as a mechanism of self-defense, lest they become overwhelmed by our industrial and commercial might. I predict that within 10 years of the nationwide implementation of this new educational system in the United States, all other nations of the world will follow suit. Given sufficient time, the dramatic improvements in American society as a result of this new educational system will spread to all corners of the earth.

I have recently discovered that a school for black children already exists in New York City's Harlem district. The school is named "Harlem Children's Zone." It was developed and is run by "Mr. Geoffrey Canada." From what I have been able to learn, the school practices some of the hypothesizes I have outlined in this book.

The school is organized and operates in a manner very similar to the educational system I have outlined herein. The success rate of "Harlem Children's Zone" has been phenomenal! President Obama has promised to create 20 more such schools, organized and operated as closely as possible to the model demonstrated by Mr. Canada's "Harlem Children's Zone" types of schools.

I could never have hoped for a better conformation of the "Wise Public School" hypothesis outlined in this book. Mr. Canada has created this miracle from an initial investment of $76 million, with an approximate $5,000 per student per year cost for 1,200 students; much less, than I have estimated. However, I am not going to change my estimate because I do not believe anyone can accomplish as much as Mr. Canada has done with so little money. It is truly a miracle!

It is my hope that, in the early stages, a philanthropic organization would take the lead in implementing this new educational system by establishing one new school in the heart of one of the poorest and most struggling school districts in the nation. This school will hopefully be constructed and administered in an area in which rates for school dropouts, drug abuse and crime are among the highest in the nation. I foresee the school as having a capacity of approximately 600 students from grades 1 through 12. I hope that some students would travel to the new school from surrounding school districts, allowing the school to constitute a true cross section of the area's population.

The school would require about 30 teachers, 12 administrative and support staff, plus 30 senior citizen and 30 college student volunteers. The salaries of the teachers, administrative and support staff would be relatively high as compared to similar positions in traditional schools, in order to attract the best teachers available.

(for an interesting video on school teacher salaries... http://www.cbsnews.com/video/watch/?id=7359538n&tag=contentMain;contentBody)

The project would require a 13-year commitment from the philanthropic organization. The first year would be spent acquiring the school facilities and hiring teachers and staff. The remainder of the first year could be devoted to selecting students by lottery from an area surrounding the school. Qualified students would have to the means to commute to the new school, since providing transportation would entail significant and unnecessary cost to the funding organization.

The cost estimate of the entire project spread over 13 years would be approximately $100 million. I have based this cost primarily on the current average salary for a public school teacher in Washington DC ($58,000). This salary would be increased by 50% in order to attract the most qualified teachers in the local area. I have estimated staff salaries as equivalent to the current average teachers' salary. The start-up cost, including funds for a building and any necessary renovations, plus other necessary materials, is estimated at approximately $4.6 million, taking into account the fact that the school will be located in an economically depressed area. Community organizations and volunteers could accomplish much of the renovation. Six hundred dollars per each first year student will be needed to provide laptop computers for all. An additional $270,000 will be allocated for new student computers each year. Another $400,000 would be required for networking the school so that each student has access to the internet in every classroom. For yearly maintenance and other expenses, I have estimated approximately $800,000 per year.

Considering that ten year cost of public education for the same 600 students (based on the current per student cost without adding inflation) in Washington DC is approximately $78 million, and that my estimate increases teachers' salaries by 50%, this project would prove a real bargain, and well within the resources of many American philanthropic organizations, as it amounts to only about $6 million per year!

The reason I so fervently hope that the pilot program would be established in such a severely disadvantaged area is because such a strategy would provide the most challenging test possible for the new system. Even modest success of the project would represent an unprecedented achievement in American educational history. If the new system did succeed to the degree I believe it can, it would represent the greatest single philanthropic undertaking in history, resulting in the most efficient use of humanitarian funds ever provided to needy recipients. The success of such a project would hasten the implementation and spread of this new educational system by generations. Its successes would constitute the greatest advance in human civilization since the advent of agriculture. Moreover, this revolution in our educational system would represent only the tip of the iceberg as compared to the radical changes in human society that would follow within a few human generations because of this first and most important step towards the Fifth Revolution.

Business in America

Human societies could not exist without business, as they provide necessary commodities for human survival as well as for human pleasure. Therefore, the Fifth Revolution cannot begin or progress without the cooperation of the business sector in pursuit of the National Agenda as identified in this book.

Business is usually defined as the production of goods and services for sale at a profit. In view of my proposition for a National Purpose, I would amend that definition to read the production of goods and services for sale at a profit in pursuit of the fulfilment of the National Agenda. In a wise human society, all business decisions should live up to two basic criteria…

1.Will it be good for the Children of America in the foreseeable future?

2.Will it be profitable and good for business in the foreseeable future?

Adding the first criterion for business decisions and practices forces for-profit institutions to weigh the implications of their decisions and practices for future generations; thereby insuring that such concerns as environmental prudence and safe disposal of wastes are of paramount importance. Moreover, by recognizing the well-being of America's children as the top priority of business and relegating the maximization of profits to secondary status, practices such as the exportation of jobs in favor of cheaper foreign labor (resulting in the loss of needed jobs at home and the exploitation of foreign laborers) will become relics of the unenlightened past.

In my opinion, the boardroom of every corporation in America should prominently display a large sign reading, "Is it good for America's Children?" Such a message could serve as a constant reminder to every board member that their primary responsibilities lie with the well-being of generations to come. An identical sign should likewise adorn the walls and presentation halls of every business whose conduct could influence the nation's future.

I believe that this can happen, once children are raised from infancy to adulthood with a firm commitment to the National Agenda. Such children, of course, will be capable of giving and receiving unconditional love and will conduct their lives according to the virtues with which they have been raised, and which constitute their character: honesty, honor, purpose, persistence, diligence, dedication, self-sufficiency, self-confidence and self-control.

Government in America

Despite popular opinion, the role of government is not to rule human society.

The actual role of government is to provide a safe and secure environment (or forum, if you will) for Life, Liberty and the Pursuit of Happiness for all citizens of the society, and for all social interaction between humans, be it business-related or otherwise.

Government's actual purpose is not widely recognized anywhere in the world, and history provides abundant evidence that its role was mistaken in the past. Traditionally, government has been considered an institution for controlling the population, often in a totalitarian and dictatorial manner, and often to the extent of attempting to dictate its subject's ideas. Even today, some governments attempt to dictate proper dress, proper diet, and even the private sexual practices of its subjects. Imagine laws that spell out how people can and cannot conduct their sex lives in private!

The role of government should never entail restricting the freedom of its citizens to act in any way they please, as long as their actions have no detrimental impact on their fellow citizens. Rather, the only fair and wise responsibility of government is to protect its citizens from the greed, bullying, sickness, madness and unmitigated evil of certain members of society, or from outside threats from foreign powers. The proper role of government is to protect the weak from the strong while guaranteeing the birthright of every citizen or resident (i.e. the right to live one's life in any manner they choose so long as their actions do not interfere with or infringe upon the birthright of any other person). This responsibility implies the government's duty to prevent a tyrannical majority from limiting or denying the rights of any minority population.

In order to explore these ideas in greater depth, we must define "birthright:"

Every human infant is born into the world in a state of complete helplessness and dependence. The care of other humans is required in order to sustain an infant's life through its formative years. It is the birthright of every human infant to enjoy unconditional love and to receive the care, nourishment and education required to reach adulthood equipped with all the skills, talents and values he or she will employ in fulfilling The National Agenda.

Every human adult, from early adulthood through maturity is entitled to the following birthrights ...

> 1. The right, upon reaching majority status, to vote for government officials in regular and special elections regardless of income, living standard, color, race, ethnicity or social standing.

> 2. The right to a good job with sufficient salary to provide decent living conditions that can be sustained above the society's defined poverty level.

> 3. The right to any available medical care required in the event of illness or accident, regardless of financial circumstances. Such medical care should be affordable to the average citizen, and it should never force a reduction in the standard of living of citizens who require it.

> 4. The right to higher education in accordance with one's individual abilities, efforts and desires.

5. The right to retain the fruits of their labor for the benefit of themselves and their families.

6. The right to privacy, protection and the sanctity of one's own home, so long as conduct within the home does not infringe upon the rights of any other member of society.

7. The right to protect themselves, their families, their possessions and the sanctity of their home by any means necessary, so long as that protection does not violate the rights of others to the same.

8. The right to petition government and receive compensation for wrongs committed against them. This includes the right to sue all wrong or perceived wrongdoers, including the government.

9. The right to amass wealth to the limits of their capability, energy and ambitions, so long as this does not deprive any other member of society of their rights. (Violations of the last clause of this right have resulted in some of the most insidious problems of modern American society. The very wealthiest 25% of the population hoards or otherwise fails to invest a sufficient proportion of their wealth in job-creating enterprises to the extent that some citizens are incapable of maintaining a lifestyle above poverty level.)

These birthrights are derived from and based upon the Laws of Nature (as I understand them) and the National Agenda which is logically derived from the Laws of Nature. This is sole Authority which should; and I believe eventually will be accepted by the majority of humans and human governments worldwide. I also believe this Authority should be recognized and recorded for posterity as an amendment to the Constitution of the United States of America.

The responsibility of any just and efficient government is:

1. To provide for military defense against all foreign attempts to infringe upon or deny the rights of any of the citizen or resident.

2. To provide a police force and criminal justice system for monitoring and controlling the daily conduct and flow of commerce and transportation, as well as for preventing, judging and punishing any and all criminal activity.

3. To protect the society's borders from illegal immigration and smuggling of contraband materials across those borders.

4. To provide a public school system to ensure equal opportunity in education so that no child is forgotten or deprived of the best education possible; education with the primary goal of preparing students to exercise character strength and wisdom in the conduct of their own lives as well as in the raising of their children.

5. To ensure that the goods and/or produce sold in the society's venues for commerce are both safe and effective. To further prevent the financial sectors of society or the very wealthy from taking unfair advantage of the less advantaged, as has, unfortunately, been accepted practice since the beginning of finance and wealth in human societies.

6. To negotiate and forge treaties with foreign nations that are in the best interests of all concerned.

7. To impose taxes on citizens, residents and businesses that are sufficient to meet the needs of fulfilling the proper role of government, but which do not exceed those needs.

8. To borrow capital when all other avenues for fulfilling the government's proper role have been exhausted. Such borrowing should include stipulations whereby the debt incurred is repaid by the generations of humans alive in the society at the time the debt is incurred.

I believe that only a government which is limited by the standards listed above can ever hope to guide its citizens and residents in the proper pursuit of the National Agenda (i.e. toward a more just, moral, happy and productive manner of living). Furthermore, I believe that the proper pursuit of the National Agenda (i.e. The Unconditional Love, Care, Nourishment and Education of all American children) should be the primary concern of all Americans and of the American government.

Democracy in America

If we sincerely appreciate and desire a free democratic government that is truly a government of the people, by the people, and for the people (i.e. the society), then we must realize that such a government is not possible under current conditions in the United States of America.

The "Golden Rule" of government (i.e. "those who have the gold make the rules") is practically a Law of Nature in this country. Currently, the outcome of political elections is determined primarily by the wealthiest 25% of the population, who own or control 87% of the nation's wealth. If you believe that wealthiest fraction of Americans donate hundreds of million of dollars to political campaigns out of pure generosity, then you have not been paying sufficient attention to national news reports. Monetary campaign donations are given in expectation that the candidate of choice will facilitate legislation favoring the best interests of the donor rather than those of the nation at large.

A truly free democratic government cannot exist so long as a political candidate requires millions of dollars in order to conduct a successful campaign for our government's highest offices. Thus, it seems to me that the only solution to the problem is to prohibit candidates from spending large sums of money in conducting their campaigns.

The majority of money spent on election campaigns is currently used to fund media advertising, such as the seemingly ubiquitous 15 and 30 second ads that are aired repeatedly on national TV during campaign seasons. Banning such ads would save candidates and their benefactors millions of dollars. This would allow less wealthy but otherwise equally qualified political candidates the opportunity to seek offices that are now virtually closed to them, and it would eliminate the possibility that our elected officials feel obligated to lobby for the interests of big business to the detriment of the common good. In an ideal democratic society, public officials represent the best interests of all their constituents and of the nation at large.

Political donations should be limited to $1000 per source of funds. The prevention of "back door" political contributions should be primary concerns of the FBI and the U.S. Treasury Department. Moreover, corporations should be constitutionally banned from contributing to political campaigns, unless those donations are equally distributed to all parties running for a particular office. It is not a proper function of business to influence the outcome of public elections. After all, corporations are not citizens but rather enterprises owned by citizens. Allowing corporations to influence the outcome of public elections amounts to granting certain individuals more that one vote, a situation that was not intended by the Founding Fathers.

The banning of commercial political advertising would force candidates to resort to less ethically questionable methods for gaining recognition and acceptance by the voters. I hope that candidates could then be judged on their personal merits and on the positions they articulate on their websites and in articles and books in the print media. Their presence in the visual media should be restricted to national debates and unbiased news reports and interviews, as well as through televised town house meetings. The number of personal appearances should be regulated in such a way that wealthier candidates do not enjoy an unfair advantage. Moreover, those ubiquitous political signs that mar the landscape of our cities, towns, and country sides during campaign seasons should be regulated or banned completely, as those who can afford the largest number of signs are always those who achieve the greatest name recognition among voters.

National Television would be required to broadcast town meetings and debates without cost to the candidates, while the government would compensate TV producers for their operating expenses in airing these broadcasts. Moreover, these programs would be commercial free and aired on all major networks simultaneously.

The television broadcasting companies would experience a loss of revenue, but then political campaign advertising does not represent a large share of television broadcasting company's income. The airways are, in fact, owned by society and just leased by the broadcasting companies. The broadcasting companies when bidding for airway frequencies would factor this loss into future bids.

In addition, the elimination of polling places staffed by human volunteers as well as voting machines that are vulnerable to tampering or malfunction in favour of direct mail or online voting would minimize the possibility of deliberate or unintentional inaccuracies in the tallying of votes. This would also contribute greatly in reducing the cost of elections to society.

The adoption of these kind of election laws would there by relieve the financial burden on political office holders, and thereby permit them to do the jobs they are elected to do rather than spending a large portion of their time and effort in raising money in order to be re-elected.

The End of Crime in America

Crime in U.S. costs $675 billion a year, according to Kerby Anderson in U.S. News and World Report. David A. Anderson of the National Institute of Justice estimates the cost of Crime at $1 trillion, including $400 billion for the pain and suffering of the victims of crime.
(http://www.leaderu.com/orgs/probe/docs/crime.html)

According to the FBI's annual report on crime for 2008 (the last year for which complete data exist) there were arrests for…

Usually not for profit crimes

Murder and non-negligent manslaughter 12,955; Forcible rape 2,258; Aggravated assault 429,969;

Total 465,508.

For profit crimes

Robbery 129,403; Burglary 308,479; Larceny-theft 1,266,706; Motor vehicle theft 98,035; Arson 14,125; Forgery and counterfeiting 90,127; Fraud 234,199; Embezzlement 21,402; Stolen property 111,319; Prostitution and commercialized vice 75,004; Drug abuse violations 1,702,537; Gambling 9,811;

Total 4,061,147.

(http://law.jrank.org/pages/12119/Economic-Social-Effects-Crime-High-Cost-Crime.
html#ixzz0ybVkiUqC)

The above demonstrates there are about 8.7 times more "For profit crimes" than "Not for profit" crimes. The former cost the USA more than $700 billion annually! If we ended "For Profit Crime," we would reduce the prison population by more than 87%!

It is possible to end "For Profit Crime" in America if we are willing to think "outside the box". I propose a simple change in the manner in which individuals and corporations conduct business . I suggest that "For Profit Crime" could be virtually eliminated if we remove cash as an alternative for monetary exchange and mandate that all commerce be conducted via an all-electronic monetary system.

There are four types of crime in modern human societies:

> 1. Crimes of passion are usually committed against the members of the perpetrator's own family or against his neighbors or acquaintances. Such crimes occur as a result of the perpetrator's losing control and resorting to violence against the object of his anger or frustration.

> 2. Crimes of insanity are perpetrated by individuals who, as a result of temporary or permanent mental impairment, were incapable of understanding the difference between right and wrong or between legal and illegal at the time that the crime was committed. Serial killers often fall into this group. Child abuse, murder, rape and aggravated assault are often perpetrated by insane individuals as well.

> 3. Crimes of omission or neglect occur when, due to failure to take reasonable precautions, the perpetrator causes unintentional harm to his

victims. Crimes such as "driving under the influence" fall into this class.

4. Crimes for profit are crimes committed in order to enrich the perpetrator at the expense of the victim. This type of crime is the most common. Included in this category are robbery, burglary, fraud, extortion, bribery, drug dealing, smuggling, tax evasion and political corruption.

The fourth class of crime, crimes for profit, is the most common. Eliminating this type of crime could be accomplished quite easily by simply eliminating cash in the conduct of all business! This could be accomplished quickly and efficiently, once Congress passed and the President signed into law a mandate to eliminate the exchange of all paper money. This law would require that all individuals and businesses in the country deposit any cash they possessed into a prior bank account, or into a new one established for this purpose. The deposited funds would then be available for exchange via "debit card", "electronic transfer" or paper check. Transactions in cash would then become unlawful and criminal

How will this system prove effective in eliminating for-profit crime?

1. The goal of any crime for profit is the attainment of untraceable and spendable paper money. Unless stolen money can be used for purchasing desired goods, no sane person would be motivated to steal it! It is difficult to trace the rightful ownership of any piece of paper money. Debit cards, however, do require that a record be made of every transaction. Every financial transaction anywhere in the country creates a bank record identifying the source and recipient

of the transaction. No sane thief would be motivated to steal if his very act of theft identifies him as the perpetrator! Drug dealers who conduct their business on the streets do not accept credit cards as acceptable payment for very obvious reasons. No sane politician or public official will accept a bribe if a clear and traceable record of the bribe could be readily obtained.

2. The act of requiring that all financial transactions be conducted via debit card, credit card or check will discourage most criminal activities. To assure that all illegal transactions could be traced, banks would be required to maintain meticulous records of the sources and destinations of all transactions. Any transaction having a suspicious source or destination would be reported to a special branch of the FBI or the Secret Service, where the transaction could be investigated. In cases where seemingly suspicious transactions are perfectly legal (as when individuals are the beneficiaries of large monetary gifts or inheritances), the matter could be easily resolved. In the case of actual criminal activity, the crime, the criminal, and the victim would be readily identifiable by bank records. These records would constitute incontestable evidence, making criminal prosecution more probable.

3. In reality, the system is already functioning to a limited extent. Most financial transactions in this country are now conducted via debit cards, credit cards, checks and electronic wire transfers. If this method of currency exchange were not already functioning efficiently, our present financial system would not exist. The wealthiest people in this country seldom employ

cash in their financial dealings. Moreover, the majority of middle class citizens in this country already rely primarily on debit cards, credit cards and checks more than they do on cash. It used to be that retail establishments would feature express checkouts for customers only using cash, because these transactions were simpler and quicker than credit card purchases. This is no longer the case. Now, with the introduction of modern card sweeping devices, it is the debit and credit transactions that are quicker and more efficient…no waiting while the cashier counts the money and makes change! It is primarily the poorest segment of society that still relies largely on cash. This is the case because the poor often fail to establish credit, or lack the necessary funds for maintaining bank accounts, which often assess fees for those who fail to maintain a certain minimum balance. I suspect that the poor would welcome the shift to electronic monetary transactions, especially if banks were no longer be allowed to penalize persons who lack the funds for maintaining large monetary reserves in their accounts. This would also give the poor access to bank services now available to the richer only. Salaries and welfare payments would electronically deposited directly into the employee's specified bank account (eliminating the need for a trip to the bank or a check cashing service in order to cash or deposit a paycheck). Both rich and poor would benefit from the simplicity and added security of a non-cash based monetary system.

5. Small businesses, which form the backbone of the U.S. economy, would benefit greatly

from the elimination of cash from society. Most businesses in this country already have the necessary equipment and electronic networking required for the cashless system. The change would reduce the cost of accounting and security for businesses by a significant factor. It would also end large scale pilfering and stealing from inventories with the intention of selling the stolen goods for profit. Small businesses would benefit sufficiently from the elimination of cash while their gain could be used to offset a significant portion of their business taxes.

6.   The most serious objections to the elimination of cash will undoubtedly relate to privacy issues. In reality, personal privacy in this country is already compromised to a greater extent than most people are aware, thanks to the internet. Perhaps the government should address violations of privacy that are already possible through online sites that promise, for a fee, to reveal information that most people would prefer remain confidential. The proposed non-cash system would never make personal financial data available to persons not specifically authorized by law to investigate such data. Banks already maintain complete records with respect to the financial status of many millions of Americans, yet few are concerned that this represents an invasion of privacy. As is current practice, the government's access under the proposed new system would be limited to trivial data in the absence of a court-issued warrant.

7. The only segment of society that currently benefits from the availability of untraceable cash is the underclass of criminals. While it is true that the elimination of untraceable cash

may be inconvenient for a few individuals, the savings of the hundreds of billions of dollars spent on crime far outweighs any inconvenience to individuals. Moreover, the elimination of the pain and suffering of crime victims cannot be quantified in monetary terms. In reality, the persons who would most benefit from the new monetary system are the poorest and most disadvantaged citizens of our country.

8. Secure Debit Cards and Credit Cards would preclude many abuses of the new system that might otherwise occur. The elimination of cash would require improvements in the security measures already in place for debit and credit card transactions. Each card will feature a recent photograph of the authorized cardholder. An additional requirement might be some means of personally identifying and matching the card to the cardholder. A simple fingerprint or iris scanner at each pay terminal should serve the purpose quite efficiently. The relative cost of adding the required equipment and software to existing equipment would be small.

I foresee no significant or prohibitive disadvantages to the proposed non-cash system. The benefits to American people and businesses are so overwhelming as to overshadow any inconvenience it might cause to a very small minority of the people. Think of what one-half of the trillion dollar savings could do for the American education system.

Reformation of the U.S. Prison System

Imprisonment has always been the most common method used by societies for the punishment of criminal offenders. The assumption has been that restriction of a criminal's freedom for a period appropriate to the severity of the crime would provide the necessary disincentive for repeat offences. In reality, just as religion has proven inadequate for building a more moral society, the prison system has proven ineffective for discouraging potential criminals, and equally ineffective in discouraging repeat offenses by criminals who have been released.

Unfortunately, the prison system in this country has proven itself counterproductive to discouraging criminality, as U.S. prisons are now infamous as breeding grounds in which hardened criminals "educate" less violent offenders, and where gang culture, drug use, and homosexual rape are common occurrences.

I suggest another strategy for deterring crime in this country. I propose that prisons be organized and administered similar to United States Marine Corps boot camps, where young, untrained and undisciplined civilians are transformed within a few short weeks into proud, disciplined and honorable United States Marines…young adults whose parents are proud to acknowledge as their own sons and daughters.

The Marine Corps' methods entail obliterating every negative aspect of the recruit's previous civilian life that can humanely be eliminated, and then re-training their de-programmed and often physically and emotionally drained charges through the rigors of 18 hour training days, six days a week. Through this total confinement and intensive training, the Marine Corps turns undisciplined civilians into members of the proudest, most accomplished, and most honorable fighting force the world has ever known. There are no gangs, drug use, criminal activity nor homosexual sex in Marine Corps Boot Camp, nor is there any escape from the humane intensity of the 18 hour rigors of daily training beyond expulsion. The recruits are sequestered in platoons of about 75 and have very little contact with anyone other than other platoon members, mess attendants, medical staff and the Drill Instructors. The recruits are mostly isolated from members of the opposite sex, and under no circumstances are they allowed physical contact with the opposite sex. In a few short weeks, these new Marines experience such a radical improvement in their personal habits and attitudes that they seem different persons from their pre-Marine incarnations! The training is extremely rigorous yet entirely humane, despite the significant personality transformation that is accomplished.

One of the harshest and most effective methods of punishment administered to Marine Corps recruits is "group punishment," in which the entire platoon is subjected to extra physical training for an infraction committed by a single member of the platoon. As one might expect, the remainder of the platoon is instrumental in convincing the errant recruit that a repeat offence would be inadvisable, to say the least!

Another discipline method is the transfer of habitually misbehaving recruits to "discipline platoons" where the training rigors are highly intensified. The discipline platoons are greatly feared and mightily avoided by all recruits.

The Marine Corps boot camp experience remains with its alumni for life. Former marines will testify to the incalculable value of boot camp training, though few would express willingness to repeat the experience under any circumstances! In a sense, Marines never leave the Corps. At the end of their tours, they simply transfer from active to inactive status. If a serious threat to our nation's security required civilian volunteers, no doubt former Marines would be among the first and most willing to risk their lives in the service of their country. As the saying goes, once a Marine, always a Marine.

Prisons administered in a manner similar to Marine Corps boot camps would be relatively inexpensive to build and maintain. A special branch of the Marine Corps could staff them, with guards recruited from among the best Drill Instructors the Marine Corps produces, and with special training and pay incentives for volunteers. Only three or four guards plus some medical and administrative staff would be required for every 75 prisoners. Training would be vocational and occupational rather than military. Each prison would include a large farm where prisoners would be required to work 6 months out of each year. The resulting produce (along with any other products produced by the inmates during their incarceration) would be consumed not only by the inmates themselves, but would also be offered for sale on the open market. The proceeds from these sales would then be used to defray the operating costs of the prisons. I believe prisoners, after 6 months of this intense work experience, could serve as able volunteers for such worthwhile services such as forest fire fighting and natural disaster relief. Such efforts would not only benefit society (particularly if Global Warming continues, increasing the risk of forest fires), but would provide valuable training to the inmates.

Prison sentences would be "indefinite" regardless of the crime and a prisoner would be released only when experts could verify that the criminal's rehabilitation was complete, and that it would be safe to release him into society. Inmates who were judged incapable of rehabilitation would be transferred either to mental institutions or to solitary confinement for life. In rare cases, sane prisoners who to pose the greatest dangers to society in the event of escape might be executed. Ideally, veterans of the new prison system would view their periods of incarceration much as former marines view boot camp: The experience would be valued as life-altering, but the veteran would not wish a repeat sentence under any circumstances.

Such a prison system would not only prove itself an effective deterrent to crime, but it would also serve as an effective strategy for rehabilitation. Prison work experience would provide valuable training for jobs in the outside world, and former prisoners might soon gain reputations as well-trained and reliable employees, altering the current public perception of former criminals as societal outcasts.

People with such experience would make excellent employees and since military salaries are now somewhat less than those of prison guards, and with the income generated by inmates, such prisons should be considerably less expensive to operate, despite their being considerably more effective at rehabilitation than our current system.

The expected 10,000 inmates that would remain after the elimination of cash exchange could be housed in a single camp with a staff of less than 500 people, yet its operating costs would be less than that of the larger prisons that exist in our country today. Such a camp could be built in the swamps of Camp Lejeune, with a major part of the active Marine Corps force available to deal with any serious disturbances

The End of the National Debt

This chapter will probably be one of the more controversial chapters in the book because I propose more specific ways to accomplish the task than in any other chapter. The simple fact is that I am not smart enough to know how the elimination of the U.S. National Debt could best be accomplished. I have included this chapter because I believe this task is one of the most important challenges facing the U.S. population and needs to be part of the agenda of the Fifth Revolution in fulfilling the promise of the new Purpose of Life.

The current U.S. national debt is over $14 trillion and is expected to grow an additional $2 to $3 trillion through the ongoing attempt to reverse the financial disaster the country now faces. How can we as a responsible society even consider leaving such an impossible burden on our children? If we cannot pay off this debt, what gives us any sense our children and their children will be better able to pay it off! Can we not see that eventually this debt will grow into unmanageable proportions unless it is paid off before the society we know collapses into utter chaos? Is that going to be our legacy to our children and to future generations? How can we have any hope for our children and their children's future if we saddle them with this unimaginable burden of debt?

I certainly do not know the details of how this debt could be paid off by the present generation; I would propose two things though ...

1. In fulfilling the National Agenda it is the present generations (the average age in America is 40) of Americans' responsibility to pay off this debt. Prior to

1961 the national debt remained under $1 trillion. The massive increase to over $14 trillion has been amassed during the succeeding 40 years. The present generation of Americans are responsible for this increase since that they elected the people who did the borrowing on America's behalf. It is interesting to note that overwhelming majority of this debt has accumulated during years when Republicans controlled both the White House and the Senate and that the largest part of that occurred under President Ronald Reagan and George W. Bush while both of the houses of Congress were under Republican control.

2. The total wealth in the United States is estimated to be approximately $56.5 trillion; 90 percent of which is owned by the government and the wealthiest 5% of the population. This 5% of the population could therefore pay off the national debt and still be far wealthier than the other 95 % of us. The top 5% of the population using one fifth of their wealth could eliminate the national debt if forced by law to do so. This is probably not an unreasonable proposition because it is this wealthiest 5% of the population which has benefited the most from the borrowing the U.S. government has done in the past 40 years. It would leave them still far, far richer than the other 95% of us. I am not going to hold my breath waiting for this to happen though.

3. As of February 17, 2009 this debt amounts to $45974.98 for each citizen of the country. I propose that the law to eliminate the national debt be a debt tax *specifically* to be used by the U.S. government to pay down the principal of the national debt and for nothing else; and that a 1 % tax be levied on the personal gross incomes and gross business profit incomes of all Americans without any deductions of any kind. This 1% tax on gross incomes would pay off the national debt and leave the nation with a prudent surplus with in less than 40 years. This will cover the life span of those

most responsible for the $14 trillion debt. For the richest 5% of Americans this would be less than an additional $1620 a year.

Further, the Constitution of the United States of America should be amended to forbid the U.S. Government from ever passing an unbalanced budget unless such deficit budgets include a sacrifice provision by which the generation of Americans alive at the time of the deficit budget would pay off any such debt incurred by the government within their life times.

In light of the fact that the great majority of this debt has been accumulated during the past 40 years, during the life time most living Americans (the average age in the U.S. is 40) and that those younger than age 40 will benefit the most from this proposal, I do not think this proposal is unreasonable or would present any great difficulty for any living person in the U.S. As a matter of fact I think it would be the wisest thing this country has ever done as a nation.

This pay down of the national debt could be accomplished by the present generations of Americans with a reasonable sacrifice as suggested above. But this could only be accomplished if the leadership we elect and sent to Washington were wise enough in the first place to realize the importance of paying off the national debt to the future of this country; and then were wise enough to convince the rest of us that it was an absolutely necessary sacrifice demanded for the future generations, especially in light of the National Agenda describe in this book. As just recently demonstrated by a significant portion of the U.S. population in electing Barrack Obama to be President of the United States of America, I believe the people of America can force such wisdom onto the leadership in Washington DC through a movement such as was demonstrated by that election. If the American people really want to change in the way Washington does things, this would be a very good place to start.

We all know that getting out of our present grave economic difficulties is going to require sacrifice. Could any sacrifice required of Americans produce such significant results as the relatively small sacrifice of one percent of our national income, being used for less that 40 years, to pay off the national debt? This is a short time frame so most Americans would live to see accomplished. Can you imagine the celebration that would take place on the day it was accomplished? Would any sacrifice we could be asked to make produce anywhere near the benefits at such a low cost to American society as the elimination the national debt would insure?

Just Distribution of American Wealth

Below are listed some references to the subject…

(http://www.huffingtonpost.com/saul-
friedman/consequences-of-unequal-d_b_674779.html

http://en.wikipedia.org/wiki/Wealth_in_the_United_Sta
tes

http://sociology.ucsc.edu/whorulesamerica/power/wealt
h.html

http://www.levyinstitute.org/research/?prog=3

http://www.faireconomy.org/files/pdf/millions_billions.
pdf)

The unequal distribution of wealth in the United States of America can only be characterized as a grave social injustice. The fact that 25% of the wealthiest people in this country own and/or control 87% (55 trillion dollars) of the wealth this society has produced and accumulated is catastrophically detrimental to the functioning of society as a whole. Moreover the system is organized in such a way that the wealthiest will continue to acquire a greater percentage of the wealth, further widening the gap between rich and poor in this country. If American society continues on its present path, in a relatively short time the wealthiest 1% will own and/or control over 99% of the wealth while the vast majority will struggle to make ends meet.   In effect, the poorest 99% will become economic slaves for the richest 1%, beholden to them for the crumbs of charity they occasionally bestow upon us.

If wealth were distributed in such a way that only 25% of the wealthiest Americans controlled only 75% of the wealth in this country, there would be no poverty in America. Keep in mind that such a distribution wouldn't even approach the almost perfect even distribution of primitive tribal societies. There are sufficient wealth and resources in this country to provide every citizen of the United States a dignified, livable income. Such an income would allow each and every parent sufficient resources to raise their children in relative comfort, health and safety and to educate those children in such a way that even the poorest among them would be capable of achieving their highest potential as productive members of society.

Of course, there is nothing unethical about the accumulation of excess wealth (i.e. wealth beyond what is required to meet the basic needs of society). On the contrary, the accumulation of expendable wealth is absolutely necessary for the proper growth and functioning of society. Only excess wealth is available to society for investment in wealth building ventures such as business development and expansion. Expendable wealth is also required for funding the research that provides the new products that are essential for societal progress. Without excess wealth being accumulated by some smaller percentage of the population for reinvestment, society as a whole simply cannot function and grow.

However, the natural tendency of the rich to get richer at the expense of the poorer segments of society in an unregulated capitalistic society is as detrimental to the progress of that society, in the long run, as would be no accumulation of wealth at all. While it is fitting and proper that the most capable and hardest working people in society receive the lion's share of the wealth produced by that society, there is a limit on how great that that share should or can be. It seems to me that we have reached and surpassed that limit, as is demonstrated by the 2008/9 meltdown of not only the U.S.'s economy, but also the world's economy.

I believe there is general consensus among leading economists that greater regulation of financial institutions both here and abroad is necessary and that some form of graduated "wealth tax" must also be implemented in order, at the very least, to settle the crushing national debt we are in the process of creating. Of course, this debt will be left for future generations to repay. How can we, as a responsible society, even consider leaving such an impossible burden on our children?

As I mentioned in a previous chapter, repaying the national debt should be the responsibility of the generations of Americans now living, since it is they who have most benefitted from the accumulation of the national debt. In addition, as mentioned previously, I believe that this would be best accomplished via a graduated "debt tax" imposed on society as a tax surcharge. This would consist of a non-deductible tax on every taxpayer's total income, with the wealthiest 25% paying the largest share. This should be done over a 40-year period (within the predictable life span of the average American living today). If properly implemented, this would mean that, at the end of 40-year debt repayment period, the United States of America would be debt free.

With regard to the re-distribution of wealth in order to establish a more just society, I do not propose confiscating a percentage of the wealth of the higher economic classes and distributing it to the less affluent, as this would neither be ethical nor feasible. It would, however, be ethically defensible to require that the wealthiest 25% invest at least 25% of their wealth in job-producing and profitable enterprises with a considerable increase in salaries associated with the new jobs. This salary increase would gradually raise the income of all workers to levels that would signal the end of poverty and unemployment in this country.

The investment of 25% of the wealth of the top 25% (approximately 13.75 trillion dollars) into job-creating enterprises would not only eliminate unemployment in this country. It would also fund the research and development of new technology that is vital to solving the world's global environmental and financial problems.

Under this proposed system, the very wealthy would still maintain control of the entirety of their wealth, but 25% of that excessive wealth would be utilized for the creation of new jobs and new technologies. The richest would be the greatest benefactors of such investments, since many of the new enterprises would undoubtedly prove to be extremely profitable.

Some of the larger projects would require government control, but would nonetheless be funded via investments of the wealthiest Americans. Examples of such projects are potential improvements in the production and distribution of electricity and the development of "bio- fuels" for powering electric plants and automobiles,

This re-distribution of wealth could be accomplished by a corporation established by the wealthiest Americans, using 25% of their wealth as start-up capital. I shall henceforth refer to the new corporation the "Wealth Foundation." Each contributor would receive stock in the new corporation proportional to their investment. In this way, the risks of corporation enterprises would be shared among all, as would the profits.

The board of directors of the Wealth Foundation would be elected from the owners who invested the capital to fund the corporation. Who could be better to direct this endeavor than the best and brightest Americans would? The board would be responsible for all decisions affecting the corporation and would be housed in headquarters as distant (both physically and conceptually) from Washington, DC as possible. The board would be required to fund a certain dollar amount of new enterprises each year.

I suggest that, by following the recommendations outlined in this chapter, we could end unemployment and redistribute wealth in such a way that would benefit all Americans, rich and poor alike. This strategy would not usurp even a portion of the resources of the wealthiest Americans, and yet it promises to raise the standard of living for all Americans and to end poverty in this country forever!

The board of directors of the We the People Corporation would
consider that the profit in which the resulted life is primarily a
function corporation CEO, and if he were found to have the
... because the life is primarily what what companies and
that he but would ... the phones that I are all decisions
... doing the profits and ... would ... because the
break-even ... that are a both is really ... and
... me has his own ... companies I be a ... to be
... the ... to profit is and ... public statement,
...

82

The End of Poverty

If the human species is to fulfill "The Purpose of Life" then it is necessary that every human born on the face of the Earth have the necessary resources and education to achieve their fullest potential as humans. This means that every family must have an income sufficient to achieve a dignified and decent standard of living. At the present this is not the case. Even in the United States of America, the most powerful and successful society in human history, approximately 15% of the population has an income which puts them below the poverty line as defined by the U.S. government. This is a deplorable fact of American life. According to statistics gleaned from the Internet, at least 80% of the world's population lives on an income of $10 or less per day. This places 80% of the world's population below the poverty line.

At the same time the distribution of wealth across the world's population is becoming increasingly more inequitable in that the richer are becoming richer while the poorer are becoming poorer. The plain and simple fact is that there is more than sufficient wealth and resources on planet Earth to raise the disadvantaged 80% of the world's population above poverty level and to allow them the dignified and decent standard of living that is the birthright of all humans.

Elevating the standard of living for the world's poor cannot be accomplished until all humans and their governments accept the Purpose of Life as I have suggested, and via a concerted effort, actively seek to achieve a more equitable distribution of available wealth and resources on Planet Earth. Hunger will decrease across the planet proportional to the success of humans and their governments in pursuing the appropriate courses of action.

As modern farming technology spreads around the world, the supply of food available to humans will increase dramatically, lowering the cost of basic necessities and thereby contributing greatly to the standard of living for the poorest 80% of the worlds population.

As the standard of living around the world increases, the birthrate among the poorest 80% of the world's population will decrease. This will eventually result in stabilization of the world's total human population at somewhat less than 10 billion. Stabilization will allow more precise predictions and allocation of the world's food production in such a way that hunger will forever be eliminated on Planet Earth.

Diseases will be virtually eliminated through several means...

> 1. As the standard of living around the world rises, the overall health of the world's population will improve dramatically as a result of better nutrition, better health habits, improved access to medical treatment, and cleaner environments.

> 2. Advances in medical technology will provide vaccines against all of the major diseases which now account for the majority of ill health and death in worldwide.

> 3. A reduction in genetic diseases, a major cause of illness and suffering today will be effected through the widespread practice of genetic counseling. It will become common practice for all potential parents to have their

DNA screened for defective genes which might lead to serious genetic diseases in their offspring. Hopefully, when couples discover they carry genes which place their potential children at high risk for genetic diseases, they will either refrain from having children, will adopt, or will seek alternative reproductive technologies that will reduce or eliminate the risk. Certainly, fulfillment of the National Agenda does not require that individuals reproduce but that they support and contribute to the proper upbringing and education of all human children.

It is should be obvious to anyone reading this little book that the fulfillment of the National Agenda as defined in this book will eventually lead to the end of poverty, hunger and disease in all human societies. Is this not sufficient reason for all humans to accept and pursue this Agenda? Is there any higher or nobler human aspiration? Is this not and has this not been the stated or implied ambition of almost all human societies since before the dawn of human civilization?

Global Warming and War

The governments and peoples of all nations on Planet Earth are now facing the first dire, truly global catastrophe in human history. The average temperature of the planet is rising at an alarming rate; and this warming, if not stopped and reversed, foretells of dramatic changes in the planet's climate. It is quite possibe these changes in the climate could lead to the end of human civilization as we know it; and perhaps to the end of human and all other life on the planet. The most learned scientists predict that if the global warming persist to its ultimate end, this planet will be nothing but a giant snow ball, covered to a depth of several miles by ice and snow, or perhaps a planet like Venus, covered with an atmosphere of metal melting hot acid or at best become as desolate and lifeless a planet as Mars now is. The bitter end lays several hundred, or maybe several thousand years in the future, but unless we stop and reverse the trend, humans will eventually become more extinct than the dinosaurs, for there will never be another life form to discover our remains and wonder with astonishment about us as we wonder about the dinosaurs. It will be just as if we never existed and all the pain and suffering, and all the joy and accomplishment of all the humans who ever existed will have been for naught!

In order to solve this catastrophic global problem all the nations of the world must come together and work diligently toward a common goal of ending the pollution of this planet's atmosphere. Never before has a problem of this magnitude faced Earth's population.

There is no possibility of any of Earth's nations avoiding the problem for very much longer. Unless something is done by all nations working together in concert, the problem simply cannot be solved. Most of the major population centers on the planet, without any help from any of their neighbors, have the capacity to prolong the global warming trend until it is too late to reverse it; just as the United States, by itself, is responsible for a significant portion of the waste that has been dumped into the atmosphere to this point.

Nor does any nation have the capability to either accomplish it alone or to force all other nations to help. The problem must and can only be solved by all nations on Earth working together in harmony toward this single goal.

This working together toward a single goal has never before in human history been required by all nations, and need we say, it has never before been attempted nor even contemplated by a majority of nations, let alone all nations.

This is the *Big Test* for humanity, we must pass the test and survive as a species or we fail and future generations of humans carry the burdens we can prevent but choose instead to increase by causing them to carry our share of the load too!

I have no doubt that humanity will pass this test, perhaps without flying colors but at the very least with a D-. There will certainly be many questions we get wrong on out first attempt but the attempt in itself is probably enough to get a passing grade, The human race is an ingenious species and has accomplished much in its short span on this planet. More over we already know what needs to be done. We need only couple that knowledge with the will, courage, effort and money that the task will require and do it. We can and must succeed because otherwise the human species is nothing but a short, insignificant hiccup in the history of the Universe.

During the process I am confident the Earth's national governments will recognize the tremendous advantage of working together in concert with all other nations will provide for their nation's people. This recognition cannot but lead to further cooperation on a global scale. The solution of humanity's other long standing and supposedly insolvable problems such as the World Economy, Poverty, and War can be solved as well. These problems can only be solved by global cooperation among all the nations of Earth just as solving global warming requires all nations to work together toward a common goal.

It is not my faith in the goodness of humanity that leads me to this conclusion, but rather my faith in humanity's s*elf interest* which cannot help but lead to the realization that the self interest of all nations and all people every where is best served by global cooperation between all nations and peoples toward the solution of all of humanity's most pressing and most common problems. As each of these intractable problems falls to the concerted efforts of all nations, all nations will become more and more comfortable with the idea and with the approach of working together with other nations in common effort.

Moreover, as each of the intractable global problems yields to the concerted efforts of all nations, the benefits that accrue to all nations will become so overwhelming that going back to the ways of *war* so common in human history will become unthinkable. As poverty shrinks into oblivion, the world economy will explode in a fruitful and controlled fashion, just as cultivated hybrid grain produces unimaginably more grain than its ancient wild cousins. The human population of planet Earth will embrace the ways of wisdom and forever relegate to history the barbaric nature of past relationships of nation with nation. The

Fifth Revolution will unfold and the Age of Wisdom will be upon all of humanity.

Join the Fifth Revolution

The Fifth Revolution will represent a new political agenda, similar to the "Tea Party" movement of the past few years. I suggest that the movement be named the "Fifth Revolution Party!" The primary objective of the movement shall be the revision of United States government and its Laws. The revision will be based on existing   Laws   of this country and a specific platform which I will specify in this chapter.

The Fifth Revolution Party will have National, State and Local Headquarters where the planning, financing and direction of the movement will be facilitated. The primary method of communication and organization among staff members shall be via email and wireless texting. Party facilities will be restricted to the minimum required to accomplish the task. The FifthRevolutionParty will also provide and maintain a web site and blogs, allowing all citizens' access to the party's functioning and relevant communications of members and interested non members. The business of the party's organizing and planning committees will be conducted via email, and with hopefully live video capability.

Headquarters will be administrated and staffed by mostly by unsalaried persons who donate their time and efforts to the cause. Every political office in the country shall have a candidate from the Fifth Revolution Party, with such candidates being selected by popular vote of the national, state and local party organizations.

Financing of the party and the movement will primarily be provided by small donations from private individuals sent by email and through corporate and foundation sponsorship, in a matter similar to Obama's political campaign. Government funding will be prohibited.

Joining the Fifth Revolution implies recognition of and firm commitment to the goal of ending poverty worldwide.

As was discussed in a previous chapter, mankind will not fulfill the "Purpose of Life" unless every child on earth has the necessary physical resources and educational opportunities for realizing their full potential…i.e. the standard of living for the entire population of the world must meet minimum standards for a decent and dignified lifestyle. Such a lifestyle is currently enjoyed by only 85% of U. S. citizens, despite the fact that our country is among the wealthiest and most politically powerful on earth. Statistics available on the internet demonstrate that 20% of the world's population subsists on an income of less than $10 per day, an income that is drastically below the poverty level for persons living in the U. S.

In addition, the sad truth is that the gap between rich and poor worldwide is ever widening. This is true despite the fact that there is more than sufficient wealth among the earth's population to comfortably sustain all of its human inhabitants

How do we achieve a more equitable distribution of the earth's resources? The answer should be obvious. Until we accept that that mankind's true goal is ensuring the future survival of our species, and that such a goal cannot be realized without a concerted effort on the part of all persons and nations living today, the malicious social ill of global poverty cannot be eliminated. On the other hand, once this objective (i.e. the re-distribution of wealth.) is identified as the wisest course of action for humanity, widespread hunger can and will be relegated to the history books.

As was mentioned in a previous chapter, we have every reason to hope that widespread application of modern farming technology will dramatically increase production of affordable food products, leading to an elevation in the average standard of living of the world's population.

Furthermore, diseases will be eliminated via the means suggested in the chapter on ending poverty.

The Platform of the FifthRevolutionParty

The following seven planks are the sole objectives of the Fifth Revolution and for the founding of the FifthRevolutionParty.

1. The establishment of laws requiring that all U.S. educational institutions be required to establish the teaching of "Parenting" and "Wisdom" as the primary objectives of their curricula.
2. The establishment of laws requiring that every American child receive a "Teaching Computer" with high speed internet access by the time they enter school.
3. The establishment of laws outlawing the use of cash as the basis for any monetary exchange in the United States, with the purpose of drastically reducing incidences of crime for profit in this country. Monetary transactions would be required by law to occur via electronic transfer.
4. The establishment of laws for reforming the United States prison system, transforming prisons into true facilities for rehabilitation.
5. The establishment of laws requiring the elimination of the National debt by the year

2051, and forever prohibiting the accumulation of debt beyond the capacity of existing generations to repay.

6. The establishment of laws which will, in effect, reduce from 87% to 50% the amount of wealth the wealthiest 25% of Americans can hold, and a more equitable distribution of the Nation's wealth. The establishment of laws requiring the elimination and/or the reduction by 50% of the staff of all government operations, with the exception of military and government entities (such as domestic law enforcement) which are required for defending the national interest.

Where to Join the Fifth Revolution

The only requirements for joining the Fifth Revolution are the desire to leave the world a better place than the one into which you were born, as well as, to the extent that you are willing and able, a commitment to expend time, effort/and or money in support of the cause. You may apply for any position in the party, from administrator to telephone volunteer, by simply contacting the FifthRevolutionParty.org member web sites. There will be a National FifthRevolutionParty web site for the country and, hopefully, one for each state and local FifthRevolutionParty organization.

Appendix

Appendix I - Human Morality and Law

When we accept "Children" as the Purpose of Life, then the entire concept of human "Morality" and "Law" changes from the age old concept of "God and Country", as the basis of Human Morality and Human Law, to the concept of one, single overriding criteria for all human decisions - "Is it good for the Children of Earth?"

This one single overriding criteria for all human decisions - "Is it good for the Children of Earth?" now provides us with a solid, provable, scientifically based foundation on which Human Morality and Human Laws can be constructed. That foundation can be simply stated as...

> 1. If it, (i.e. Anything), is good for the all Children of Earth, then that thing is morally "Good", "Right" and "Virtuous".
>
> 2. If it, (i.e. Anything), is not good for any of the Children of Earth, then that thing is morally "Bad", "Wrong" or "Evil".
>
> 3. The connotations, (i.e. degrees) of "Good", "Right", "Virtuous", "Bad", "Wrong" or "Evil" which can be applied to anything is the extent to which each individual decision under consideration effects all the Children of Earth.

In consideration of this, we can now throw out all previous moral tenants of human society; and on this foundation, we can construct new moral tenants that include only those old tenants that meet the new criteria. We can construct new moral ethics that include only those old moral ethics that meet the new criteria.

I would suggest that the highest moral virtue to which a Human can aspire is the ability to give and receive unconditional love; and that the highest moral ethics to which a Human can aspire are honesty, honor, purpose, persistence, diligence, dedication, self-sufficiency, self-confidence and self-control. I suggest this because these are the virtues and ethics a human must have in order to properly raise their Children in a manner such that they are able to reach their highest potential as human beings; and have the best capability and opportunity of achieving the Purpose of Life.

In fact, we can throw out all of the old Human Law and construct a much simpler Human Law that only includes those Laws that meet the new criteria. Moreover, we now have a foundation on which to base any new Law which insures that all future Laws are unquestionably "Good," "Right" and "Virtuous." Especially if the humans responsible for making the Law have the ability to give and receive unconditional love; and that they have achieved and practice on a daily basis those highest moral ethics to which a Human can aspire: honesty, honor, purpose, persistence, diligence, dedication, self-sufficiency, self-confidence and self-control.

What is reality and why do humans seem to actively avoid understanding reality? The best way to begin is by defining the word. The Wikipedia free encyclopedia (http://en.wikipedia.org/wiki/Reality) is available online and is accessible to everyone who can access the internet.

Wikipedia not only defines reality in several different ways, but it also includes an in-depth discussion of the concept as well as historic references to mankind's search for reality and "truth." It also provides great insight as to why humans often deliberately avoid reality .

The following two sentences comprise the best possible definition for our purposes: From the Wikipedia free encyclopedia…

> *"Reality is the state of things as they actually exist, rather than as they may appear or may be thought to be. In its widest definition, reality includes everything that is and has being, whether or not it is observable or comprehensible."*

It should be noted that human reality as it exists today, including all of the globe's social problems, are largely the result of the actions of humans existing today. Almost all of the world's problems are the result of *"well-meaning but misinformed"* human activity.

I would like to illustrate this idea this with the best analogy I have been able to construct:

> "Reality may be thought of as a giant hollow sphere made of impenetrable steel, with no windows or doors to gain inside access from the

outside. Reality consists of everything enclosed by the sphere and therefore it has no contact or communication of any kind with anything outside the sphere. If you inhabit the sphere you inhabit reality. The entire Universe is contained within the sphere. If anything can be identified as living outside the sphere, it can be described as fantasy, a fabrication of human imagination. Now, while the fantasy portrays the outside, it cannot be actualized, nor can humans interact with it in any way except in their imagination. Nothing outside the sphere is reality. It is human imagination!"

Some people exist in a fantasy world of their own creation: (http://en.wikipedia.org/wiki/Schizophrenia) from Wikipedia...

"The idea of being in touch with Reality is integral to the notion of schizophrenia, which has often been defined in part by reference to being "out of touch" with reality. The schizophrenic is said to have hallucinations and delusions that concern people and events *that are not "real."*

Approximately 2500 different Gods have been described and worshipped during recorded history, in addition to an indeterminate number prior to that time. This suggests that God beliefs may have actually originated as the schizophrenic imaginings of early Homo sapiens that persist until today.

Is it possible that the Aztec-feathered serpent God "Quetzalcoatl" actually ever existed in reality, or did it exist only in the imaginations of the Aztecs who worshipped it? Did the highest Deity of the ancient Greeks, Apollo actually exist?" Nevertheless, even if the old Gods of Mexico and Greece were pure fabrications, these fantasies were of fundamental importance in the construction, organization, and functioning of those two very different cultures.

If this is the case, could it not be possible that modern Gods are likewise founded entirely in the imagination of humans who existed long ago, and that they were perpetuated by the generations who followed in their footsteps, re-defining and re-characterizing the old Gods to suit their purposes as history unfolded

What if it could be demonstrated that a particular modern God...perhaps one acknowledged by the reader as "real," doesn't actually exist? After all, humans once firmly believed that the earth was the center of the solar system, and this belief was a fundamental component of religious beliefs at the time. How would life change for a person who had once believed in God to suddenly discover his God did not exist in reality?

A moment's thought should convince the reader that nothing with respect to reality itself would change for the former believer, since any contact that believers might have imagined they had with their God existed solely in their own minds.

The overwhelming evidence is that no God has ever communicated with any human. In fact, the books of Christianity and Judaism state that no human shall ever know the Face of God.

> Exodus 33:20: "And he said, Thou canst not see my face: for there shall no man see me, and live."

If you research the "Face of God" you will find many references to many different scriptures which address the fact that man is incapable of understanding the "Nature" of God, or of "communicating directly" with

God. The Word "Face" is used as a synonym for "Nature" in this context.

God certainly did not answer the Jewish people, His "Chosen People," in their prayers for salvation from the hell of Nazism. If, as the Bible recounts, He destroyed the whole world and two little ancient towns because their people were evil, why would he allow Hitler to destroy six million of his faithful followers? Clearly, if the God of Judaism were capable of interfering in the affairs of humans, he would have done so in Nazi Germany, since the Judeo-Christian God is both omnipotent and omni-benevolent. One might even ague that the inherent self-contradiction provided by the historical fact of the holocaust is logical proof that this God simply does not exist: Either he does not exist as described, or he does not exist, period.

Since reality includes everything that exists, there is not, nor can there be, more than one reality. One possibility is that religious reality is a component of human reality. We certainly cannot deny that human religions exist, and have existed since the beginning of recorded history. If this is true, human religions should not be immune from the same kind of scrutiny (i.e. questioning) by science and all humanity that we apply to any other aspect of human reality.

Why is it that humans possess both intelligence and instincts for survival? Would not any God expect humans to utilize the gifts that most religious people presume originate with him? If God made us, he made us to be intensely curious creatures, so it seems He certainly would expect us to investigate and question every aspect of our existence, including the claims and beliefs of our religions as they relate to our world and ourselves.

No definition of reality would prove acceptable to the vast majority of religions since it would necessarily exclude all supernatural Gods and all things supernatural. (Some forms of modern paganism are a possible exception to the rule that religions entail belief in the supernatural.) By definition, the supernatural is "above nature," i.e., it does not exist in nature, and therefore information about it cannot be accessed via human sensory organs. It can be accessed only via the human imagination. Ergo, God and the supernatural exist outside the sphere of reality.

It is instinct that causes humans to seek the "purpose" or reason for everything around them. This is one of humanity's most powerful survival instincts, allowing early man to survive in jungle and savanna environments. We possess neither fangs, claws nor a tough, armored outer layer. In the jungle we were entirely defenseless except for our intelligence and curiosity (i.e. the drive to understand the "why" of everything). As any parent will verify, children between the ages of three and five are particularly curious, incessantly asking "why?" This is because they instinctively seek a reason and purpose for everything in their environment. Intelligence is the survival mechanism that drove the evolution of pre-humans to Homo sapiens. This instinctual need to know "why" is especially insistent when a human individual considers his or her own mortality.

If we are indeed intelligent beings, should not we be concentrating on the Laws of Nature, laws that have remained constant throughout the history of the Universe, rather than on imaginary beings whose characteristics differ greatly depending on the historical period, culture, and level of sophistication of the believer? With respect to Christianity, and most other religions, the only evidence that the "Word" is truly the word of God is the Word itself! This is a prime example of circular or tautological logic, and therefore amounts to a logical fallacy. In no other area of human thought would such logic have persisted, largely unquestioned, for millennia!

Humans have great difficulty with the concept of reality, to the extent that asking 100 people for a definition would probably result in 80 substantially different answers, ranging from "reality is what actually exists," to "reality doesn't actually exist…what seems real is only an illusion."

Actually, there can be only one reality, but there are 6.8 billion different perceptions of that reality. We all perceive reality as distorted and filtered through our senses, then integrated with, and modified by our previous experiences. This means that reality is perceived and understood differently by each and every human on the planet.

Humans avoid the concept of a single reality for three primary reasons...

1. Humans are extremely reluctant to admit or acknowledge error. When religious persons encounter a fact or an idea that contradicts their distorted perception of reality as it relates to their religious beliefs, they simply close their minds, refusing to even consider the contradiction, lest it cause a disturbing shift in their worldview. For many, the potential discovery that their parents believed and taught mistruths might prove particularly unsettling.

2. Most children who are brought up in religious homes are raised to believe that some truths can be known only by divine revelation, and those truths, which cannot be

revealed by science, should not be questioned, or modified in any way. In fact, many human societies have been founded on the idea that questioning the reality of certain accepted concepts constitutes the crime of heresy. Heresy was punishable by death in many cultures throughout history, and in some countries the practice persists to this day. While the crime of heresy applies only to certain concepts, children are discouraged from questioning any idea that their society has agreed upon as descriptive of "reality." Fairy tales, Santa Claus and the Easter Bunny are examples of fables that condition our children to accept some fantasies as real.

3.   If a person accepts reality as the basis of Life then they must question their comfortable concepts of God and eternal Life. Even if such questioning is not punishable by death in this life, many religions teach that "lack of faith" will result in eternal punishment, which will be inflicted after earthly life ends. In addition, and perhaps more importantly, human beings are highly social creatures, who are evolved to function best in a community of like-minded individuals. It goes without saying that life will be much easier for humans who don't "rock the boat," but accept without question the common beliefs of the community. (Nevertheless, it is the outcasts of our communities…heretics, wise men, and futuristic thinkers…who are often most responsible for human progress.)

(From Wikipedia, the free encyclopedia. "*Homo sapiens*: Latin: 'wise man' or 'knowing man'). (http://en.wikipedia.org/wiki/Human)

> "Humans have a highly developed brain, capable of abstract reasoning, language, introspection, and problem solving. This mental capability, combined with an erect body carriage that frees the hands for manipulating objects, has allowed humans to make far greater use of tools than any other species. Mitochondrial DNA and fossil evidence indicates that modern humans originated in Africa about 200,000 years ago. With individuals widespread in every continent except Antarctica, humans are a cosmopolitan species. As of May 2010, the population of humans was estimated to be about 6.8 billion."

(For those interested, there is a very interesting article about human development and culture that can be accessed through an internet search for "The Physical Characteristics of Humans." (http://www.wsu.edu/gened/learn-modules/top_longfor/phychar/01_intro_culture_human.html))

Early humans were faced with a huge dilemma! Their instincts prompted them to seek and find a reason for their mortality and a purpose for their lives, and yet the solution was elusive. They simply lacked the knowledge to solve this problem. Similar to their universal instinctual fear of the dark, humans also have an instinctual fear of ignorance, i.e. not understanding the "why" of existence. In early humans, this fear amounted to a highly adaptive survival mechanism, since lack of knowledge could prove fatal in the face of dangerous non-human predators.

Humans are, of course, the cleverest animals. When explanations for important observations are lacking, humans are quite capable of imagining the explanations, convincing themselves of the truth of those explanations, and then passing them onto their naturally trusting children as unassailable truth. Parents are highly reluctant to admit they do not have the answer to any of their children's "why" questions, because they do not want to lose their children's faith and trust in them as omniscient and wise mentors. Perhaps early human mothers and fathers are ultimately responsible for inventing the Gods as a response to their children's "why" questions. Perhaps their answers were eventually integrated and incorporated into the lore of the society as a whole.

To understand why humans exist, early humans invented immortal Gods, all powerful beings who created and controlled the universe; and who punished all humans who did not accept and obey God's (i.e. their Supreme Father's?) words. They also invented the "Word," which was their God or Gods' directives to humans, usually delivered directly by a God to a human representative, as the Christian God is supposed to have delivered the Ten Commandants to Moses. The Word was devised to compel succeeding generations to follow the same directives, in a manner that would be less amenable to change than strictly oral transmission. Heaven was invented as a reward for those who followed the Word, and Hell for those who disobeyed.

The attractiveness of this dogma to early man cannot be denied. Those who conformed and believed the acceptable view of reality were rewarded with a blissful eternity. Those who did not conform and who did not believe were relegated to the most painful eternity imaginable…a raging, never-ending fire!

These ideas are readily acceptable to impressionable toddlers, who instinctively imagine their parents to be unerring dispensers of the truth, and who are eager to please those parents! The Hell most children fear with greatest dread is the loss of their parents' love. This makes perfect evolutionary sense, of course, since the loss of a young child's mother often meant death for that child in primitive human societies.

Once devised and accepted by society, "the purpose" must be enforced so that the society functions as a unit in support of the purpose. The best method for enforcing such a purpose is to claim that it originated with God himself. Thus, it makes perfect sense that heresy would become such an inexcusable crime in so many societies that have existed since the dawn of man. Questioning authority with regard to "the purpose" might lead to the heretic's discovery that what is dispensed as the "Truth," i.e., as a component of reality, is actually a human invention. Since the purpose is the foundation on which society is built, negation of that purpose would destroy that foundation, and the society itself might crumble.

Consider the extent to which religious beliefs influence the foundation of society in the present day United States. Our currency features the words "In God we trust." The laws of our land are founded in the Ten Commandments, as the recent controversy over a monument to these commandments prominently displayed in a public justice building attests. Much of our education system is based on ideas that originated with religion as well. There is no question" Religion has been an integral component of nearly every human society that has existed since the beginning of civilization.

One of history's most glaring examples of the extreme tactics society will employ in defending the tenets of its religious beliefs is provided by Galileo, the founder of the scientific method (a procedure that has proven indispensable for learning truths about nature and its laws). Galileo was a very intelligent gentleman who was very highly regarded by his society and by much of the civilized world as it existed at the time. He was renowned for his art, his research, his inventions, his buildings and his great intellect. Galileo employed scientific techniques to demonstrate that the Sun was the center of our solar system and that the planets orbited around it. He published his findings in a book that the Catholic Church condemned as "possible heresy." Galileo's Sun-centered solar system contradicted the "Word" of God, which insisted that the Earth was the center of the solar system. Galileo was arrested; tried and convicted, forced to recant his published data, and spent the rest of his life under house arrest. Only his renown and his many friendships with highly respected individuals prevented his execution.

As it has turned out, of course, Galileo's description of the Sun-centered solar system described reality and the "Word" was proved wrong in that regard. Although Galileo's work was quickly proven and was soon accepted by the scientific community of the time, the Church has not yet edited the Word nor did it clear Galileo of heresy and apologize until the year 2000. [the Roman Catholic Church doesn't take the Bible literally…so it considers any incorrect scientific references to be merely allegories for conveying moral truths.]

Thus, the "Word" and the tenets of religion that are claimed to be the Word of God, delivered directly to humans by God, and therefore "infallible" and "unquestionable," are, in fact, human fabrications which are therefore very much fallible and questionable. After all, only one proven falsehood in the Word is sufficient to render the entire Word questionable. In fact, the Bible and all the different "Words" of the various faiths are replete with beliefs that are not consistent with the actual reality that humans inhabit. Most humans are aware, at least subconsciously, that this is why the crime of heresy arose in the first place. In fact, many religious doctrines are contrary to many human instincts.

These many different, contradictory, "Infallible" and "unquestionable" Words could not possibly be the "Word of God" unless that Word was intended to confound humans, a nonsensical, illogical supposition. Nevertheless, societies based on these *words* simply refuse to acknowledge the inherent inconsistencies and rationalize them as analogies, allegories, or concepts too mysterious for human comprehension.

At this point, the reader might ask, "What's the problem? God seems a reasonable solution to mankind's problems."

The following is an analogy that best conveys my own reasons for believing that religion and God are not optimal solutions to the human problem:

> *Human societies have been attempting to erect a magnificent giant skyscraper (i.e. Society) in the midst of a desert, without extending the foundation of the structure to the bedrock (i.e. reality) below. Hence, they have been attempting to erect a stable structure on a foundation of shifting sand. It is, of course, obvious, that a tall building cannot survive on such a shifting foundation. Eventually, it will crumble and fall.*

The multitude and diversity of human Gods was a result of the fact that, by the time humans evolved to point where they were capable of inventing Gods to solve their "why" dilemmas, they had already migrated all over the planet and had become isolated from one another, precluding the transfer of ideas between them. Thus, each group invented God independently and, of course, each group created a different scenario for their God and for creation. Is this not definitive proof that all human Gods spring from human imagination rather than divine inspiration?

Consider that, according to renowned historians Will and Arial Durant, there have been about 2500 major Gods worshiped by various societies all over the world. With more than 2500 different creation myths and more than 2500 different methods for worshipping and serving God, it is very apparent that using religion as a foundation on which to build a civilization is tantamount to constructing a skyscraper on shifting, drifting, rolling and churning sand. History speaks to us very clearly with respect to those societies which based their culture on religion. Most are extinct, while the ones that have survived have somewhat adapted to changing times. Nevertheless, modern religions retain many of their ancient beliefs, beliefs founded on imagination rather than reality. Societies that are built on a shifting foundation are doomed to eventual self-destruction.

It bears repeating: Reality is the bedrock foundation on which human societies must be built!

We must not be too judgmental with respect to our God-inventing ancestors. After all, mothers and fathers must respond in some way to their children's incessant "why" questions! Humans have a remarkable capacity to convince themselves that fantasy is reality, so we cannot even convict them of spreading deliberate falsehoods! In actuality, God and religion were very clever inventions, because they solved very real

dilemmas for which there appeared to be no "real" solution at the time. The fact is that until about 190 years ago, the human species simply did not have sufficient knowledge for understanding the real Purpose of human existence. Of course, the events of note were the publication of Georges Cuvier's "The Animal Kingdom:
(http://en.wikipedia.org/wiki/Georges_Cuvier) and Charles Darwin's "The Origin of the Species." (http://en.wikipedia.org/wiki/On_the_Origin_of_Specie s)

Although this knowledge has been available for nearly two centuries, its implications have not been widely accepted. This book is an attempt to elucidate the implications of the theory of evolution and the fossil record to the purpose of human life, as we can best interpret it within the boundaries of reality as it actually exists, rather than as we imagine it to be.

It is not well known that the totality of human knowledge of reality doubles every 5 to 7 years (depending on which expert is making the estimate). This means that the information to which the average person has access is about one million times (2 to the twentieth power) more than the information available to his grandparents 100 years earlier. Modern man now has access to several trillion times (1,000,000^20) more than his cave dwelling ancestors.

The significance of this exponential growth of knowledge is that every book written before the twentieth century relied on information that was severely limited as compared to information available today.

Thus, when ancient books were written, humanity was severely handicapped, in that only a tiny fraction of the knowledge that exists today was accessible to them.

This is particularly true in the case of the great religious books, which professed to represent the transcribed Word of God himself.

The reality of human existence I have identified in this book is based on the latest scientific information available to humanity, and thus differs significantly from the Realities and Purposes presently accepted by most members of most human societies. Most religious believers consider the purpose of human life to be service to God. The purpose I propose in this book is revolutionary, and thus would significantly influence the structure and functioning of human societies, in ways that would prove beneficial for the future of humanity.

In fact, I believe that accepting human reality as a foundation for civilization has the potential to solve nearly every human problem!

This is not supposition, speculation, nor fantasy. It is logic combined with recorded and verified history, together with scientifically proven facts that anyone could verify for himself if he so desired or dared. It is my belief that, if the suggestions outlined in this book are universally implemented in this country or world-wide, the Utopia for which man has been searching since the dawn of civilization may finally be realized.

Appendix III – Clue to the Purpose of Life

When I was a young man, I was very interested in philosophy and read just about every book on philosophy and religion I encountered. To me, religion is simply an alternate form of philosophy. Throughout my life, I have spent considerable time pondering the question "What is the Purpose of Life?" I have read that humanity has been asking that same question since the beginning. I suspect that every mature, rational human being who has ever lived has also observed the exquisitely beautiful night sky, with stars sparkling like diamonds on black velvet, and pondered the same question. The solution to that question probably represents the most pursued and yet elusive nugget of knowledge in all of human history.

At age 26, I experienced what I now consider a revelation. It occurred to me that if a God existed, and if that God intended for humans to have a specific reason and goal towards which they should strive from birth to death, then there had to be a clue somewhere on Earth that would lead us to the unequivocal truth with regard this "real" human purpose. Without some mechanism for rationally discerning that purpose, it may as well not exist for humankind! An analogy might be a person in authority who asked you to go fetch something, but refused to identify that which you must fetch! If the person fails to properly acquire that unidentified something, the result is the cruelest form of punishment that can be imagined. Of course, such a scenario is preposterous in that it contradicts not only logic, but also virtually every concept of justice that humankind has ever acknowledged!

If nothing else had been discovered during the 560 years that followed the invention of the printing press, one thing is clear; the Universe and the Laws of Nature are anything but illogical. Although the Universe at first glance may seem utterly chaotic, the Laws of Nature are, in fact, completely constant, extremely reasonable, and infallibly logical. The only reason we perceive chaos in the Universe is because of the different densities in different areas of the Universe and the fact that old stars die and explode while new ones are continually being formed from the debris. The fact that The Laws of Nature are immutable explains why science and the scientific method can exist, and can discover truths about reality. The Laws of Nature provide the absolute and perfect standard by which everything real can be measured and quantified. The mathematical Laws of Nature also provide the absolute and perfect means whereby measurements are made and quantifications and conclusions reached. Thanks to the Laws of Nature and science's ever expanding knowledge of those laws, we humans know and understand, with considerable accuracy, the events that constituted the Big Bang some 13.8 billion years ago, including the changes that occurred during the first one millionth of a second of the event. Were the Laws of Nature not immutable and constant across time and space, it would be impossible for us to understand the Big Bang and our eventual appearance on earth. The scientific method and the entire field of science could not exist without these absolute and unchanging Laws of Nature.

If it were not for basic science and its more practical counterpart, applied science, none of the technical advances that have led to our modern electronic world would or could have been realized. The human life span would still stand at 25 years, were it not for the fruits of science.

At age fifty I experienced yet another revelation. I discovered the long lost "Clue" to the Purpose of Life, while watching Carl Sagan's TV program "Cosmos. The "Clue" was the "fossil record of Life" here on Earth, which dates back 3.8 billion years. The reason it had been hidden in such plain sight for so long was due to the fact that humanity simply had no foundation for understanding the significance of the fossils they uncovered, not what they might imply for understanding the origin of life. The significance of fossils was not understood until the development of the scientific field of Paleontology in 1817, with the publication of "The Animal Kingdom" by Georges Cuvier. The field of paleontology became established in the 18th century as a result of Georges Cuvier's work on comparative anatomy, and developed rapidly in the 19th century, leading to Darwin's "On The Origin of Species" in 1859.

The true significance of the fossil record as it relates to the Purpose of Life is still not recognized by the scientific community at large. There have been three books of which I am aware that have proposed that "propagation" is the only Purpose of Life. However, no one, to my knowledge, has advanced the concept as it relates specifically to humankind, i. e. that humankind's true purpose is the care, nourishment and education of all of the earth's Earth's children.

For more than 20 years, I have pondered the best method for publicizing and utilizing my discovery. I expected to someday open a newspaper or hear a news report in which a member of the scientific community would report reaching the same conclusions I have presented in this little book. When the true Purpose as I have identified it is finally published as the opinion of a highly respected and renowned scientist, I suspect that it will cause such a stir that it will be widely reported in the news. Ideally, this book would be published as a paper in a journal devoted to the philosophy of science, but not being a scientist, I could not hope to present my thesis via this route.

Over the 24 years since I discovered the clue to the Purpose of Life, (and consequently the real Purpose of Life), I have tried to imagine what human society would be like if the Purpose of Life (as I have identified it) were to be accepted and pursued to the same degree that the religious Purpose of Life is now accepted and practiced? I cannot help but conclude, based on my own experience and my engineering background, that every aspect of human experience would be greatly improved. It is my contention that acknowledging and pursuing the Purpose as I propose it would lead to the elimination of Global warming, the energy crisis, the national debt, war and preparations for war, crime, poverty, hunger, disease, racial tensions and radical fluctuations in the Earth's financial systems ... *Forever*!

I have found, through years of talking to people about my discovery that the first essential step for understanding the Purpose of Life is to understand human reality and the Laws of Nature. To understand human reality we must recede 13.8 billion years into the past and to the beginning of the Universe. Far too few people are aware of the latest scientific knowledge with respect to the origin of the Universe. Most educated humans are aware of the Big Bang theory, but few are aware of the events that took place during the first few microseconds following the Big Bang.

Appendix IV - The Big Bang

Of all the concepts I will present on these pages, understanding the Laws of Nature is most crucial. You cannot comprehend reality unless you also understand (or at least acknowledge as real and absolute) that The Laws of Nature are the forces that control and limit everything that exists in the Universe. They are immutable and constant across time and space and limit all that exists in the Universe. Indeed, the Laws of Nature, in many important ways, resemble the Gods of all the major religions of the world! These Laws have been discovered, clarified and verified by thousands of dedicated, highly educated and intelligent scholars and scientists, mostly since the invention of the printing press in 1450, or only about 560 years ago. These laws have been studied and tested in every imaginable and conceivable way. They have been shown to be the most constant phenomena in the Universe. In fact, The Laws of Nature may be the ONLY ABSOLUTE in the Universe! These laws differ from human Laws in that, unlike human Law, the Laws of Nature CANNOT be broken, period! This is the most important aspect of reality that humans must realize and understand.

If something is allowed by the Laws of Nature, it can be part of human reality.

If something is forbidden by the Laws of Nature, it CANNOT be part of human reality. It can only be imagined and not manifested. Some concrete examples of this are the facts that no two solid objects can occupy the same space at the same time, matter and energy cannot be created, only transformed into some other kind of energy or matter, nothing in the Universe can change in any way in the absence of some energy or force which effects the change, and finally, NOTHING can move faster than the speed of light.

The Laws of Nature existed, and were operative, from the instant the Big Bang occurred. It is surprising to me that the scientific community understands this fact but does not seem to recognize its significance. Our understanding of the Big Bang absolutely confirms the existence of the Laws of Nature from the beginning. The scientific community has no clue as to what, if anything, existed before the Big Bang, nor do they have a clue as to how the infinitively hot and dense, sub atomically sized bit of energy/matter came to exist, or from where it came. If anything existed before the Big Bang, it was displaced by it, unless it was somehow shielded from the tremendous release of energy/matter the Big Bang expansion produced. (Please take note that if anything did exist before the Big Bang, it would not have been real to humans because the Laws of Nature dictate that nothing in nature could survive such tremendous heat and pressure.)

The Big Bang occurred when a very tiny, tremendously hot and tremendously dense something exploded in an ever-expanding wave of extremely hot quark-gluon forming plasma. Within the first microsecond of the expansion the plasma had cooled sufficiently for quarks and subatomic particles to form and acquire mass. Proof that the Laws of Nature were in effect at the same time lies in the fact that only the types of quarks and subatomic particles which now make up the Universe survived the first microsecond into the big bang and every one of the trillions upon trillions of the six types quarks and other subatomic particles was identical to every other quark of the same type; the other subatomic particle types were also identical within each type. All the matter we can find in the entire Universe was created in that first microsecond. The Universe then was less than 600 meters in diameter. If anything else was created during the Big Bang, it was not sufficiently stable to exist in this reality, causing it to vanish, or it is something we humans have not yet discovered and quantified.

(Dark Matter and Dark Energy are two of the things science has discovered but about which we have little knowledge beyond our awareness of their existence. Dark Matter makes up 80% of the mass of the Universe. Dark Energy opposes gravity and is causing the Universe to expand faster than the forces of gravity would allow.

About 1 second into the Big Bang, the expanding mass had sufficiently cooled that quarks and gluons could combine into protons, antiprotons and neutrons. This process lasted for about 10 seconds. At this point in the Universe's history, it was approximately 6000 kilometers in diameter, slightly less than twice the size of our moon. Again, trillions upon trillions of identical protons, neutrons and antiprotons were created. Fortunately, for us, about 1% more protons were created than antiprotons because, being identical except for their equal and opposite electrical charge, protons and antiprotons destroy each other when they come in contact. The Universe we see today consists of that 1% difference in the number of protons and anti-protons created.between 3 minutes and lasting for only 17 minutes into the Big Bang, about 33% of the protons fused together to form helium and a far lesser number fused to form lithium and a very few other heavier elemental nuclei.

By 377,000 years into the Big Bang's expansion, all the hydrogen, helium and lithium nuclei had recombined with electrons to form the elements hydrogen, helium and lithium and a few other heavier elements.

From this point on, the hydrogen, helium and lithium were drawn by gravity into immense clouds of gas that eventually formed into galaxies. The clouds further divided into massive star types where gravity compressed the gas until it was sufficiently hot and dense for fusion to occur. The hydrogen, helium and lithium fused together to form the heaver elements. These massive stars consumed the hydrogen, helium and lithium and at very fast rate compared to a much smaller star like our Sun, a rate of perhaps millions of years as opposed to the billions of years that it will take for our Sun to dissipate. These relatively short-lived stars very quickly exhausted their fuel and become Supernovas. During the Supernova stage, the heaver elements formerly created within the massive star, from hydrogen, helium and lithium are fused into the heaviest elements known. The Supernova is an explosion that ejects all known elements throughout space. This resulting debris mixes with clouds of hydrogen, helium and lithium that haven't yet formed into stars. When a new star forms, it is composed of all the elements from these dense clouds, as are any planets that form around it. Every element that comprises the human body as well as any planet we inhabit was created in the belly of these giant stars during the first billion years of the Universe's existence. We actually are composed of the stuff of stars, and we really are connected in a very fundamental sense to the entire Universe!

We should note that with 100 billion galaxies composed of 100 billion or more stars each (more stars than there are grains of sand on Earth) making up the entire Universe, every proton, neutron and electron in the Universe is identical to every other proton, neutron or electron in the Universe. All are made up of the same types of quarks and gluons and arranged in identical manners. In addition, all span 13.8 billion light years (the distance light travels in a year at 300,000 meters or 186000 miles per second) of space and time. Can there be any doubt that some force was at work in creating these basic identical particles of the Universe? That force can be summarized as the Laws of Nature.

The significance of the fact that the Laws of Nature were operative from the instant of the Big Bang is that, from that instant forward, almost everything in the Universe was preordained! The only thing that was not preordained and predictable at that point was the positions of all the elements, galaxies and stars within the galaxies. Some would argue that, if we had had sufficient knowledge, the positions of all the atoms of all elements could also be predicted. However, I doubt that. The randomness of the position of the individual atoms, and the constant reuse and random redistribution of atoms is absolutely necessary for the Universe to exist in the form it does and the distribution of the matter in the Universe is so random that it would be impossible to predict any position. The randomness of matter dispersal in the Universe is also necessary; otherwise, life on this planet would not exist.

At the instant of the Big Bang, Life on some planet orbiting some Sun in some unknowable Galaxy somewhere was preordained. Life, and eventually "intelligence" was destined to appear, according to the laws of "probability." Given the proper circumstances, the raw material and sufficient "time", anything that is possible has a probability of happening equal to "ONE". This implies that, from the beginning of time, the Laws of Nature dictated that life, and eventually intelligent life, were destined to appear at some time, on some planet.

We can state this as fact for the following reasons...

1. We know without doubt that Life and Intelligent Life are possible. There can be no doubt because Life and Intelligence (not wisdom) do indeed exist on this planet we have named Earth. We humans are the grand winners in the greatest lottery ever conducted in this universe!

2. The Universe is composed of giant clouds of hydrogen, helium and lithium. Randomly dispersed within these clouds are all the elements that can possibly be created in the center of an ultra massive star, from the smallest massed element, hydrogen, to the heaviest massed element produced in massive stars, uranium. The elements are created, from the lightest to the heaviest, by fusing one or more protons onto to a lighter element. The atomic numbers of elements are the same as the number of protons and electrons the atom contains. The atomic numbers are sequential for Hydrogen (1) through Uranium (92) which is the heaviest element produced naturally. Each heaver element is formed by fusing one additional proton to the nuclei of the next lightest element. Heavier elements through atomic number 137 are possible but only a few of these have been synthesized in scientific laboratories. Different elements are created during a supernova in proportions equal to the temperature and pressure of fusion required for the fusion process. The entire process of Supernova formation and creation of all the elements heavier than carbon require less then a second. Once initiated, the temperature and pressure first rises and then lowers as the Supernova runs it course. Each different element fuses together at different temperatures and pressures. In the process of exploding, the Supernova expels the elements at nearly the speed of light and, as a result, the elements are

scattered far and wide. Each atom continues along a straight line until it is slowed and captured by the gravity of a giant cloud of hydrogen, helium and lithium, which is probably already dispersed with the debris of earlier Supernovas. The dispersal is totally random.

3. So, the result is a giant gas cloud which is heavy with the all the elements which exist in nature. At some point there will be a disturbance in the cloud and it will collapse into a star, pulling lesser amounts of the gas into planets which will orbit the star for its entire life. However, most of the hydrogen, being the lightest element in the cloud from which our solar system originated, was pulled into the Sun. All of the planets are composed of all of the elements in the same proportions (with the exception of hydrogen) that existed when they were created-- i. e., at the time when these elements were randomly dispersed. Our own solar system was created in just this way some 4.6 billion years ago.

4. The Universe is chaotic because every atom in the Universe is positioned randomly, and because many stars at the end of their lives become novas or supernovas which distribute masses of new elements throughout the Universe. Moreover, new stars and solar systems are continuously forming. Again, keep in mind that that the distribution of elements is random!

5. The chaos on Earth is caused by weather, earthquakes, erosion, volcanoes, floods, ice, fire and many other forces. What is significant in this regard is that all the elements needed to create life are continuously mixing, moving and bumping into one another. Therefore, we have a chaotic planet in a chaotic Universe and the "possibility" that the exact

elements which are required for the formation of life are continuously and naturally being stirred and mixed, in the proper proportions for supporting life as we know it!

6. Given the chaotic conditions on Earth 3.5 to 4 billion years ago and the possibility that life could arise, the appearance of life on earth was inevitable! Moreover, the conditions here on earth dictated that, once life originated, it would continue to evolve into different life forms, and that those life forms would survive and propagate, with some forms surviving for longer periods than others do until, eventually, intelligence (the ultimate survival tool) resulted. The final step in humanity's evolution will, I believe, entail widespread acquisition of the wisdom necessary for utilizing our naturally endowed intelligence to facilitate and accelerate our further evolution. I believe the problems our species currently face can only be solved by applying the wisdom that nature's example has provided.

It is important to note that, while it is true that a watch found lying in the desert does imply a watch maker, since the metal pieces that constitute the watch must be machined and assembled. After all, the Laws of Nature do not allow metal to form itself into any shape under any circumstances. In the above scenario of Life, however, there is no supreme "watch maker" that was required in order for life to appear spontaneously on Earth (although any human watch maker, and thus any watch the watch maker produces, are the result of those forces). Life, after all, is the inevitable result of the mixing of the proper elements in the proper proportions, (a naturally occurring event on a planet such as ours), and for a sufficiently lengthy time that all possible combinations of elements, in every possible sequence, will occur with virtually 100% certainty.

The formation of only ONE living cell was required in order to initiate the process of biological evolution that eventually would populate the entire Planet with a seemingly endless diversity of living forms. So, even if the first living cell didn't have the appropriate composition to survive and reproduce itself, the elements would continue to mix until another formed. (It is quite possible that life formed several different times with several different organizations while other life forms already existed. The only requirement for life on this planet is the formation of DNA or RNA as part of the living organism's means of propagation.) The biochemical's that made up the most primitive living organisms were allowed by the Laws of Nature to self-assemble upon coming into contact with one other-- otherwise Life would not have been possible.

In fact, recent discoveries have shown the existence of some simple amino acids in outer space. Amino acids are the building blocks of proteins, which are essential to life on earth, as we know it. Every multi-cellular organism on Earth originates as a single cell that replicates itself, followed by replication of the daughter cells, until the entire multi-cellular adult organism results. While environmental influences help shape the resulting organism, there is no need for a conscious "watchmaker" to direct or interfere in the process. Since all multi-cellular organisms can trace their origin to a single-celled ancestral organism, there is simply no need to postulate a supreme watchmaker to explain the origin of any form of life on this planet.

In summary, a God was not necessary to account for the arrival of life on our planet. Life originated as a consequence of the Laws of Nature, which are part and parcel of the Universe, and which dictated that life would form and propagate on some planet somewhere in the Universe. Thus, life was preordained by these laws and therefore was inevitable! The creation myth is superfluous… it is unnecessary to account for the existence and the evolution of the universe, the earth, or life on earth. The truth may not be appealing to people who like to imagine an anthropomorphic being zapping the universe into existence. However, in my opinion, there can be no more marvelous or awe-inspiring story that the one with which reality has presented us…and it has the irresistible advantage of corresponding to the truth!

Appendix V - The Purpose of Human Life

Why is it essential that we identify a Purpose of Human Life? A moment's reflection should be sufficient to convince the reader that human beings are purpose-driven beings: We do virtually nothing without a purpose, whether that purpose be conscious, unconscious, stated, implied, or ignored. We have been endowed by nature with multiple instincts, and these instincts drive our purposes. We engage in sex for pleasure, for procreation, and to express love. We labor in order to provide life's essentials (food, shelter) for ourselves and for our families. We watch television in order to acquire information about our world and also for entertainment

In order for a society to be successful (i.e. produce just, moral, happy and productive citizens.) that there must be some commonly acknowledged purpose of life, a common goal which is accepted and practiced by the majority of the society's citizens.

> A little less than 8 million Americans, representing 3.1% of the U. S. population is in prison, on probation or on parole for failing to follow the National Purpose. The incarceration rate for the U.S. is the highest among advanced nations.
> (http://en.wikipedia.org/wiki/Incarceration_in_t he_United_States)

While the overwhelming majority of the population of America adheres to the Purpose of Life as stated in the Declaration of Independence and the Constitution of the United States, very few acknowledge that these two documents do define the Purpose of Life for all Americans.

The Declaration of Independence clearly states the National Purpose of the United States of America. The second sentence reads…

> "We hold these truths to be self-evident, that all men are created equal, that they are endowed by their Creator with certain unalienable rights, that among these are life, liberty and the pursuit of happiness."

The closing sentence reads…

> "And for the support of this declaration, with a firm reliance on the protection of Divine Providence, *we mutually pledge to each other our lives, our fortunes and our sacred honor*."

If this isn't a declaration of National Purpose, I cannot imagine how one could be stated more clearly or more unequivocally.

Now while the Declaration of Independence boldly invokes the authority and assistance of a Creator (i.e. a Deity), it was in fact written by humans in a human forum, and agreed upon by the majority of immigrants occupying colonial America. This majority agreed to the extent of armed revolution, which meant death for many. Their purpose was undoubtedly as stated in the Declaration of Independence, as was the purpose of all the Union soldiers who fought and died in the civil war and all succeeding wars in which Americans have been engaged. Many paid the ultimate price for their defense of the National Purpose. The original document is enshrined in Washington DC for all to see.

In view of these considerations, how could anyone deny that the National Purpose is not of vital importance to its citizens and to the nation as a whole?

If this is true, wouldn't it be possible for today's citizens, living in more enlightened times than those of our ancestors, to re-define and improve upon the National Purpose as conceived by our Founding Fathers, a purpose that will better serve the needs of society in promoting justice, morality, happiness and productivity? In doing so, we need not stray from the ideals advanced in both the Declaration of Independence and the Constitution. After all, the Founding Fathers allowed for later refinement of the Constitution, via amendment. Since not all Americans today worship the same deity, and an increasing proportion of the population acknowledges no deity, wouldn't it be prudent to examine and amend our national purpose using our intelligence and rational foresight instead of the questionable authority of a deity of unknown and unknowable characteristics?

I believe the unequivocal answer to these rhetorical questions must be YES! Thus, I propose a change to the U.S. Constitution which will clearly state the following National Purpose:

The National Purpose of America is the *Unconditional Love, Care, Nourishment and Education of all of America's children*; This purpose can be demonstrated scientifically without any reference to any Deity. The wisdom that demands this conclusion can be deduced from the scientific evidence that exists in the 3.8 billion year fossil record of life on Earth. The function of life is to reproduce itself, in such a way that each succeeding generation is better adapted for survival than the parent generation.

Since the words "function" and "purpose" are interchangeable according to both the English dictionary and the English thesaurus, I believe it is reasonable to conclude (as many renowned sciences have done) that the purpose of all life forms is simply "survival in order to propagate the species".

Humans, of course, are not exempt from the same Laws of Nature that apply to all living things (despite the fact that many people consider mankind to represent evolution's crowning achievement.) Thus, mankind's firm place in the unity of nature implies that he is not exempt from the same purpose that applies to all living creatures. It is true that man's level of intelligence is unprecedented in the biosphere. Perhaps ironically, it is this distinguishing characteristic of mankind that renders the purpose even more applicable to man than to any so-called "lower animal." Unlike most other mammals, and thanks to the oversized human brain, a human infant must be born in a very immature state, before their brain reaches proportions that would prevent it from passing through the birth canal. Moreover, humans are more reliant on learning that their non-human counterparts. Thus, unlike the young of any other mammal, human infants and children require fifteen years or more of *Unconditional Love, Care, Nourishment and Education.* Otherwise, children cannot and will not mature into *just, moral, happy and productive citizens of society.*

I believe the bulk of humanity's problems can be traced to child abuse. I am not referring exclusively to the most egregious forms of abuse, in which children are physically and mentally tortured by parents who are supposed to love them, but to more subtle forms of abuse, perpetrated by well-meaning parents who may truly love their children, but who are misinformed as to the proper strategies for excellent parenting.

I also believe the best method for solving virtually all of humanity's problems is to educate children in the art of Parenting and the art of Wisdom before they themselves become parents.

Appendix VI - The Wonder of Wisdom

Wikipedia, the free encyclopedia defines wisdom as:

"a deep understanding and realizing of people, things, events or situations, resulting in the ability to choose or act to consistently produce the optimum results with a minimum of time and energy. Wisdom is the ability to optimally (effectively and efficiently) apply perceptions and knowledge and so produce the desired results. Wisdom is comprehension of what is true or right coupled with optimum judgment as to action. Synonyms include sagacity, discernment, or insight. *Wisdom often requires control of one's emotional reactions (the "passions") so that one's principles, reason and knowledge prevail to determine one's actions.*"

Please note that knowledge is the basic requirement of wisdom! Please also note that Plato's formulation of knowledge is "justified true belief." Also, note that humanity has yet to reach a consensus in defining the words "knowledge" or "reality." Thus, it is not surprising that humanity all too often lacks the necessary wisdom for solving its most difficult problems. What is surely needed is an optimal strategy for making the wisest decisions possible, if human societies are to achieve their maximum potential as institutions for ensuring the continued well being of our species.

It should be obvious to the reader that few if any humans always act with wisdom as described above. We might question why this is so…After all, it seems everyone should desire to act wisely, if only for purposes of self-interest. Why is this? Surely the answer lies in the final, highlighted sentence ("so that one's principles, reason and knowledge prevail to determine one's actions.")   No human religion ever conceived on Earth could withstand the scrutiny demanded by this definition of "wisdom." We have been taught since birth to avoid the most fundamental aspects of reality, as they are heretical or in opposition to the church and to society. Under such scrutiny, all fables and myths that are presently taught as realities would be reveled for what they actually are...products of *"human imagination!"*

It is virtually impossible for any religion ever conceived on Earth to pass the test of reality imposed and demanded by the application of wisdom. Certainly no religious creation story can be shown to correspond to reality, and this fact by itself would invalidate (or at least cast into doubt) all of the fables and myths that are presently taught as "The Word of God."

Unless humanity can provide a suitable alternative, abandoning religious myth and fable could prove disastrous for humanity. Religion provides people with a sense of purpose, false as that purpose may be. If we discard religious purpose, our very nature demands that we replace it with a suitable, and hopefully better, alternative.

The personalities and characteristics of a good parent allow wisdom to develop naturally as a child matures, but only if those children are provided with guidance by way of example during their earliest years.

Furthermore, the personalities and characteristics of a good parent demand that the parent strive to serve as a suitable example for the child's growth and development at *all times* and in *all situations*!

Of course, it is not reasonable to expect that anyone could ever be a perfect parent, who never erred in providing guidance and example for his child. But this is not a serious flaw in the strategy. Perfection, after all, is not the goal--raising wise and healthy children, both physically and mentally, is the goal. Human infants and small children are remarkably resilient with respect to occasional parental errors. It is repeated and continuous abuse that warps children's minds. The personalities and characteristics of a good parent forbid such repeated and continuous abuse, as the chapter on parenting makes clear.

It is inspiring to imagine a world in which the majority of humans consistently acted with wisdom in every aspect of their lives. It seems obvious to me that virtually ALL of mankind's most pressing problems would be solved if wisdom were a defining characteristic of all humans, and if all humans strove towards a common goal, recognized and agreed upon by the application of wisdom. It would be hard to imagine a single human problem that would remain intractable when such an application of knowledge, energy, and intelligence is applied to its solution.

The most appealing aspect of this idea is that it can be easily accomplished. All that is required is that we educate our children in wise and proper parenting skills in order to break the cycle of error that is bequeathed from parent to child, generation after generation!

I have broadly outlined in the chapters of this book the steps I believe humanity must take if we are to solve the most serious problems that are now facing humanity. I have not attempted detailed procedures for achieving this goal, because I do not believe that any one individual has sufficient knowledge to do so. Solving humanity's problems will require a concerted effort of the world's population. It is my hope that this book will provide a wake-up call for the best and brightest of humanity to lead "The Fifth Revolution" towards a brighter future for humanity.